Not As We Ought

A Lutheran Reflects on the Nature of Prayer

Charles St-Onge

To My Wife, Deborah

For all her love and encouragement,
and for helping me learn how to pray.

"For we do not know what to pray for as we ought, but the Spirit
himself intercedes for us with groanings too deep for words."
- Romans 8:26

Contents

Introduction

Any visitor to a Christian or even a secular bookstore can not help but notice the quantity of books on prayer. What is a Christian to make of all these books? Do they all essentially say the same thing, or are there significant differences in theology from one author to the next? A Lutheran may be forgiven for asking whether there is a particularly *Lutheran* understanding of prayer, and where one might go to find out about it.

Luther certainly valued prayer highly. Each of his catechisms contains an exposition of the Lord's Prayer. He wrote a book on prayer for his barber, tracts on the prayers of the church, and constantly enjoined the necessity of prayer. He himself wrote "we should and must pray if we want to be Christians."[1] One may therefore safely conclude that prayer was not of an incidental importance for Luther.

Neither should prayer be of incidental importance to any Christian. Latin American theologian Fernand Ménégoz wrote, "A theology which (can) neither justify nor give a constructive interpretation to the possibility and meaning of prayer (is) in a state of near-collapse."[2] How one understands prayer defines not only how one understands the Christian life, but also how one understands God. "The notion of God, in so far as it is characteristic of the discourse of the believer, is both one of the clues to understanding the meaning of prayer and one of the problems for those standing outside the religious community."[3] If one's understanding of prayer reflects one's understanding of God, and one's relationship to God, then a theology of prayer takes on a great importance.

Since Lutherans claim a distinctive understanding of God and his work, as well how he continues to relate to humanity, Lutherans must also have a distinctive understanding of prayer. This is not to say that only Lutherans, of all Christians, are able to pray properly and effectively to God, anymore than Lutherans claim that they alone have been saved by Christ. However, it is to say that the Lutheran understanding of prayer, as in the case of the Lutheran understanding of the sacraments, of God's election, and a number of other points of doctrine, is unique within the Christian community.

Luther's writings themselves display an understanding of prayer that is noticeably different from the views held by many contemporary writers, even within the Lutheran confession. The saving of the sinner by a righteous God in Christ Jesus is programmatic for Luther's understanding of prayer, as it is for all his theology. Prayer arises naturally out of the regenerated saint brought to faith in the Gospel through the preached Word and the sacraments. It is the response of the believer to the God who continues to save him from sin, the devil, and ultimately from death itself.

In many contemporary writings, however, prayer takes on other meanings as well. Chief among these is the view that prayer is itself a means of grace, used by the believer to build and strengthen his relationship with God. Nowhere is this approach to prayer more obvious than in the so-called "Sinner's Prayer" given to unbelievers by some Evangelical Christians as both a means to, and a sign of, conversion. Most Evangelical Christians believe God has given free will to humanity in spiritual matters, and prayer therefore plays a prominent part in the conversion and life of the Christian. This view of prayer tends toward the "magical," seeing prayer as a means to curry favor and acquire blessings from God. Prayer becomes a form of spiritual exercise with corresponding spiritual (and occasionally material) benefits.

Another common perspective is that prayer, as a form of "communication with God," is useless. God, after all, is omniscient, omnipresent, and omnipotent, and so has no "need" of our prayers. Prayer then must be something other than "talking" to a Supreme Deity. Proponents of this position see prayer as action in the world. To pray is to be actively working to accomplish God's will. Any other definition would be to reduce God to the status of a divine gift-giver, a heavenly Santa Claus constantly waiting for our updated wish list.

In between Luther's view and these two latter views fall most authors of books on prayer. They tend to emphasize one or another of these three positions. In the end, what occurs is a tendency to relegate prayer to the same status as a magical incantation or potion, or to make of God a distant and transcendent supreme deity with little interest in "speaking" to his creatures. Luther avoids both of these extremes by retaining God's sovereignty, and emphasizing his sovereignty for us, as our Savior. It is this saving relationship that forms the basis for all prayer, in Luther's view.

In the following chapters, several contemporary writings on prayer will be examined, with a view to comparing them with Luther's own writings and views on prayer. In so doing, the contrast between Luther's own perspectives and those of other authors will be drawn out. The differences are not necessarily consequential in and of themselves. But they do demonstrate more fundamental disagreements on the nature of God, his work in Christ, and his relationship with both believers and unbelievers alike.

---

[1] What Luther Says. Ewald Plass, ed. (St. Louis: Concordia Publishing House, 1959), 1076
[2] Perry LeFevre. Understandings of Prayer. (Philadelphia: Westminster Press, 1981), 9
[3] LeFevre, 59

Chapter 1: Martin Luther on Prayer

The Lutheran Church takes its name from the man that the Arts and Entertainment channel listed as the 3rd most important individual of the 2nd millennium, Martin Luther. While churches of the Lutheran confession of the Christian faith do not claim any infallibility for Luther's non- confessional writings, these writings do provide important insights into the man who played such a pivotal role in the 16th century reformation of the Christian church. Most Lutheran churches bind themselves to Luther's Small Catechism as a clear exposition of Scripture, for example, and other more conservative Lutheran bodies also bind themselves to his Large Catechism as well as his Smalcald Articles. Nonetheless, Luther's writings are not Holy Scripture, although they might be put on the same level as the apocryphal writings of the Old Testament, many of which Luther described as containing much good and being well worth reading.

Luther's theology of prayer flows out of his understanding of God and of God's will toward humanity. In his younger years, Luther saw God as a distant judge who required strict obedience from his creatures. Luther understood the righteousness of God spoken of by Paul in Romans 3:21[a] as being a righteousness he must exhibit in and of himself toward his creator. As Luther, who was an exegetical professor at the University of Wittenberg, studied and taught the Scriptures his understanding of God's righteousness began to change. He came to see this righteousness as a gift given freely to all people by God's grace. This gift is appropriated by faith, not by the works proscribed by the church, whether masses, pilgrimages,

---

[a] But now the righteousness of God has been manifested apart from the law, although the Law and the Prophets bear witness to it— (Ro 3:21). All texts, unless otherwise noted, are from the English Standard Version or ESV.

veneration of the saints, or the meriting or purchasing of indulgences. The Gospel - the Good News - is that humanity has been granted perfect righteousness as a gift from God, for the sake of Christ's atoning life and sacrifice. This understanding of the Gospel became the core of Luther's theology, and Luther interpreted all other doctrines and dogmas in light of this understanding of the Gospel. Any exploration of Luther's understanding of prayer must then begin with a brief look at his understanding of the character and will of God in light of this Gospel.

Luther and the Character of God

Among the works that Luther considered his best, and one of the few he felt was worth keeping, is his Bondage of the Will, his answer to Erasmus' Diatribe on the Freedom of the Will.[1] In this work, Luther defends the belief that God elects Christians to faith through the Gospel, solely by his grace and without any worthiness on the part of Christians. Luther shows that God works in two distinct ways in the world. First, there is God as he works all in all. Nothing occurs without God's knowledge, and nothing comes to pass without God either actively or passively willing its occurrence. This is God as he works through society and through creation to restrain evil and enforce his Law. This is also the God who elects only a few out of the masses to faith in the Gospel, while leaving others to the condemnation they have earned by their sinful rebellion against him. These decisions and actions of God are not knowable by humanity, either through the use of reason or through some special revelation; they are "hidden" from view. This "hidden will" of God is "not to be inquired into, but reverently adored, as by far the most awe-inspiring secret of the Divine Majesty, reserved for himself alone and forbidden to us..."[2] The unbeliever, when looking for God's activity in the world, is confronted only with his inscrutable "hidden will."

Second, however, there is God as he has revealed himself in the Scriptures. This is God as he would have all humanity know him: the God of grace and mercy, who desires that "all men be saved and come to the knowledge of the truth" (1 Timothy 2:4). This God, the Father, the Son, and the Holy Spirit, has given to us all that he is and has. Luther makes this clear not only in *The Bondage of the Will* but also in his "Confession Concerning Christ's Supper" of 1528:

> The Father gives himself to us, with heaven and earth and all the creatures, in order that they may serve us and benefit us... The Son...gave himself and bestowed all his works, sufferings, wisdom, and righteousness, and reconciled us to the Father, in order that...we might also know and have the Father and his gifts... The Holy Spirit comes and gives himself to us also, wholly and completely.[3]

God as he would have us know him is a loving Father, who sent his Son into the world because of his great compassion for humanity, and who subsequently sent the Holy Spirit that people might be brought to faith in his Son's atoning work on humanity's behalf. There is nothing that this God has withheld from humanity; he is a God who wishes only to bestow good gifts on his redeemed creatures (Luke 11:13[b]). Only the Christian knows this "revealed will", as God's Word is open to him through the same Holy Spirit who has brought him to faith.

There are then, for Luther, two wills within God, as he is viewed

---

[b] If you then, who are evil, know how to give good gifts to your children, how much more will the heavenly Father give the Holy Spirit to those who ask him!" (Lk 11:13)

from the human perspective. The first will is God's sovereign will over all creation, which is not to be inquired into but simply acknowledged and adored. The second will is God's gracious and saving will toward his creatures, which is the will that God has fully and openly revealed to all people in his Word. The tension between these two aspects of God's character - his revealed will for his creatures and his will that remains hidden from their view - plays an implicit role in Luther's understanding of prayer. In prayer we do not attempt to peer into or manipulate God's hidden will. Prayer, instead, flows out of God's revealed will. Prayer, its objective, and its content do not fall into the realm of the hidden, but rather into the realm of the objective grace and promises of God toward humanity accessible by faith through the Scriptures.

Luther and the Nature of Prayer

Prayer and Faith

If prayer belongs in the realm of the objective, revealed will of God, then faith must by necessity precede prayer. Only once a person is brought to faith in Christ is she able to pray rightly. Without faith wrought by the Holy Spirit, a person prays without any confidence that God will hear. God is not God for them, but merely an impersonal something. But once faith is created by the Spirit through the preaching of the Gospel, and especially in baptism, the believer places her trust in God, confident that God wants to give her every good gift, and that God himself has commanded her to ask for these gifts. Luther writes in his Large Catechism:

> All who are outside the Christian church, whether heathen, Turks, Jews, or false Christians and hypocrites, even though they believe in and worship only the one, true God, nevertheless do not know what his attitude is toward them.

They cannot be confident of his love and blessing. Therefore they remain in eternal wrath and damnation, for they do not have the Lord Christ, and, besides, they are not illuminated and blessed by the gifts of the Holy Spirit.[4]

This view that faith is necessary for prayer is reiterated in the Lutheran Confessions. In his Apology to the Augsburg Confession, Philip Melanchthon wrote: "prayer without faith is not prayer."[5] This should not be viewed, however, as making something within the Christian - his faith - merit an answer to prayer. Rather, the need for faith points to the one who creates the faith and sustains it with his indwelling, the Holy Spirit. The Holy Spirit himself makes prayer on the part of the Christian possible. So even in the moments of weakest faith the Christian is pointed not to his own failings but to the comfort that even his weak faith demonstrates the Spirit's work in his life. The Spirit then, intercedes for the Christian "with groanings too deep for words" (Romans 8:26). The very fact that Christians are commanded by God to boldly approach him as "Father", and ask for every help in time of need, demonstrates that prayer is grounded solidly in God's gracious will toward humanity. In the words of David Scaer, "The concept that the Christian can pray only with the Spirit's aid again accentuates the centrality of God's grace in Luther's theology."[6] Luther wrote, "Wherever a Christian is, there the Holy Spirit is, who does nothing else but pray constantly...Therefore you cannot find a Christian without prayer, just as you cannot find a living man without a pulse."[7]

Prayer and Good Works

If prayer follows faith, and prayer is commanded by God, then is prayer a "work" done by the Christian? For Luther, prayer is more or less a troisième route between the traditional "means of grace" - preaching and the sacraments - and good works done for one's neighbor. On the one hand, there are places in Luther's writings and the Lutheran Confessions where prayer is spoken of in the same way as good works. Philip Melanchthon wrote in the Apology to the Augsburg Confession, "We believe that God's glory and command require penitence to produce good fruits, and that good fruits like true fasting, prayer, and charity have his command."[8] Prayer is listed as a "good fruit" that flows forth from the regenerate Christian, along with fasting and charity. He also wrote, "It is false, too, that by its own strength reason can love God above all things and keep his law, truly fear him, truly believe that he hears prayer, (and) willingly obey him..."[9] Here Melanchthon lists prayer as one of the responses to God that the Holy Spirit alone, utterly apart from reason, can produce. Just as the unbeliever cannot keep God's law or fear him - in other words, have faith - so too it is impossible for the unbeliever to prayer with true confidence.

Luther himself speaks of prayer on more than one occasion in the same way as Melanchthon. In his Smalcald Articles, Luther wrote of Cornelius, the God-fearing Centurion to whom Peter was sent to preach. He said that Cornelius' prayers and alms were acceptable to God in this faith even before his baptism, because he had heard the Word of God concerning the coming of the Messiah through the Jews.[10] Luther's listing of alms and prayers together suggests again some connection between the good works of the Christian towards his neighbor and the Christian's prayer to God. Alms are given to the poor as a Christian's response to God's requirement that the poor be cared for (Matthew 25:35[c]). Prayer, in the same manner, is done because God had commanded that we pray (Matthew 7:11[d]).

---

[c] For I was hungry and you gave me food, I was thirsty and you gave me drink, I was a stranger and you welcomed me... (Mt 25:35)

[d] If you then, who are evil, know how to give good gifts to your children, how much more will your Father who is in heaven give good things to those who ask him! (Mt 7:11)

Prayer and Grace

In other places, prayer is spoken of in a manner similar to the preaching and teaching of the Word and the benefits of the sacraments. It is spoken of as a means of obtaining grace, as a way through which the Holy Spirit works to create and sustain faith. Melanchthon wrote the following in the *Apology to the Augsburg Confession*:

> Ultimately, if we should list as sacraments all the things that have God's command and a promise added to them, then why not prayer, which can most truly be called a sacrament? It has both the command of God and many promises. If it were placed among the sacraments and thus given, so to speak, a more exalted position, this would move men to pray. Alms could be listed here, as well as afflictions, which in themselves are signs to which God has added promises. But let us pass over all this. No intelligent person will quibble about the number of sacraments or the terminology, so long as those things are kept which have God's command and promises.[11]

Both Baptism and the Lord's Supper have been commanded of God, and have attached to them the promise of the forgiveness of sins. Prayer, likewise, has been commanded by God and also has great promises attached to it. Christ assured us that if we asked, we would receive (Matthew 7:7[e]), and that our heavenly Father would certainly give the Holy Spirit to anyone who asked (Luke 11:13[f]). Therefore, in Melanchthon's view, prayer could be considered to be not only a means of grace but also a sacrament, if one were to define a

---

[e] "Ask, and it will be given to you; seek, and you will find; knock, and it will be opened to you. (Mt 7:7)

[f] If you then, who are evil, know how to give good gifts to your children, how much more will the heavenly Father give the Holy Spirit to those who ask him!" (Lk 11:13)

sacrament as anything commanded by God with promises attached to it.

Luther himself says that the Holy Spirit can speak in times of prayer. He wrote that if during prayer good thoughts come to us, we ought to "make room for such thoughts, listen in silence, and under no circumstances obstruct them. The Holy Spirit himself preaches here, and one word of his sermon is far better than a thousand of our prayers."[12] Here Luther speaks of prayer as a vehicle for the communication of the Holy Spirit. Taken together with Melanchthon's statement, this would seem to suggest that prayer is not a good work, but actually a means through which God creates and sustains faith by the work of the Holy Spirit, as he does through preaching and through the sacraments.

Prayer as the Response of Faith

To phrase the question in common Lutheran terminology, is prayer a good work or a means of grace? Is it perhaps both? And if it is both, what does this mean for Luther's understanding of salvation by grace through faith alone? We must remember at this point that for Luther, prayer is almost interchangeable with faith, and that faith itself is a gift from the Father, created through his Holy Spirit. For Luther, "Prayer is not many words, as Christ says in Matthew 6:7[g], but rather a turning to God frequently and with heartfelt longing, and doing so without ceasing (1 Thess. 5:17[h])."[13] What else is faith but a turning to God with heartfelt longing? David Scaer wrote, "Prayer indicates that the Christian has not given up hope and his willingness to seek help from God...In his helplessness the afflicted can go no place but to God for aid and assistance. Prayer is the plea

---

[g] "And when you pray, do not heap up empty phrases as the Gentiles do, for they think that they will be heard for their many words. (Mt 6:7)

[h] ...pray without ceasing, (1 Th 5:17)

for aid."[14] Prayer must be treated alongside, and in a manner not altogether different from, faith.

Faith is required to appropriate the righteousness of God earned by Christ, made available to us purely by God's grace. Faith is the medium by which grace is received: the means of passively receiving the righteousness of Christ on the part of the believer. Just as the reception of a gift is never considered a work on the part of the receiver, so the receiving of the grace of God through faith cannot be considered a "work", even though it is happening within the believer. The Holy Spirit through the Word has created the faith within the believer in any case, whether through preaching or a sacrament. Since the faith worked by the Holy Spirit through the Word receives the graciousness of God through Christ, it can also be said that prayer, being an exercise of faith, also receives the grace of God. In this sense prayer is, indeed, a "means of grace." However, in the sense that it is the Word of God alone, in preaching, teaching and the sacraments, that conveys the forgiveness and grace asked for in prayer, prayer is not strictly speaking a means of grace. Raymond Surburg writes, "The grace and forgiveness for which we ask in prayer is conveyed through the Word of God and the Sacraments. The latter are the means of grace, not prayer."[15]

One way to understand this view of prayer as a troisième route is to distinguish between prayer in the wide sense, and prayer in the narrow sense, as understood by Luther. In the wide sense, to the extent that prayer is based on and contains the Word of God, the Spirit can indeed grant forgiveness of sins in prayer, the same as he does in preaching. This is the sense in which Luther understands it when he speaks of the Holy Spirit preaching during prayer. It is also the sense in which Melanchthon may well be thinking of prayer when he speaks of it being a possible "means of grace" in the Apology. However prayer in the narrow sense, as the response of the

Christian in faith to the Word of God, is not a means of grace, but an effective and obedient asking for the grace which God graciously grants through the Word given in preaching and the sacraments.

But what about the sense in which prayer has been spoken of as a "good work"? It is true that God has commanded us both to pray and to do good works toward our neighbor. Prayer is something that God calls forth from Christians as a fruit of the faith created and sustained in them by his Spirit. Luther wrote this regarding the everyday work of the Christian:

> There is a saying ascribed to St. Jerome that everything a believer does is prayer and a proverb, "He who works faithfully prays twice." This can be said because a believer fears and honors God in his work and remembers the commandment not to wrong anyone, or to try to steal, defraud, or cheat. Such thoughts and such faith undoubtedly transform his work into prayer and a sacrifice of praise.[16]

But here again we see the connection between faith and prayer. What makes the good works a "prayer and a sacrifice of praise" is the faith of the one doing the work. Such a faith is not merely an intellectual assent to doctrinal propositions, but a living and active trust in the Father of our Lord Jesus Christ. This living and active trust - this faith - is at the heart of prayer. Just as the Words of Institution make Christ's body and his blood available under the bread and the wine, so does faith transform ordinary work into a prayer to God. Prayer as a good work is prayer understood in its narrow sense.

We come then to Luther's core understanding of prayer. Prayer is the response to God of a living and active faith present in the believer, empowered by the Holy Spirit. This response is characterized by a radical trust in God's promises. Prayer, we might then say, is faith in motion, where the object of our faith is the Father who sent his Son into the flesh to redeem the world, and sent his Holy Spirit to create faith in that Son. Prayer is the response of faith to the God who has given us all that he is and has. This response of faith is such that it takes God at his Word, namely, at his promise to give good gifts to his children.

If faith is the receiving medium which "breathes in" God's good gifts, then prayer is the "breathing out" of the trust of the Christian in that same God. To push the analogy a little further, one might say that the Holy Spirit working through God's Word is the carbon dioxide in the air that regulates our breathing. We breathe in God's Word through faith, and exhale the same Word back to God. Every human being must both breathe in and breathe out to live; one cannot choose to do only one or the other. And so Luther can rightly say that there is no faith without prayer. Just as the breath going out from a man on a cold winter's day indicates that he is alive, so the prayers of the Christian show a living faith and trust in God.

The command to pray, then, is much like the command to partake of the Supper, the command to be baptized, and the command to hear God's Word. These are not statements of Law, but "Gospel imperatives." French theologian Jacques Ellul captured this idea well. He called God's requirement that we pray a command, as distinct from a Law. "Obedience in Christ," he wrote, "is the opposite of a duty or obligation."[17] He also wrote, "What is understood in the commandment is a promise."[18] Comprehended in the command to pray is a promise that God will hear our prayer, and a promise that our prayers will be answered. For Luther, to pray in faith is to pray with expectation and with confidence. "In other words: 'Whatever good thing you lack, look to me for it and seek it from me, and whenever you suffer misfortune and distress, come and cling to me. I am the one who will satisfy you and help you out of every need. Only let your heart cling to no one else."[19]

Prayer as Petition

For what, then, shall we pray? Should we come to God with all trust and confidence that he will supply everything our hearts' desire, no matter how trivial? Here we encounter another important aspect of Luther's theology, his recognition that all humans are wickedly sinful (Genesis 8:21[i]). Although by faith we are righteous in the eyes of God, and as believers we are a new creation, our old nature remains (2 Corinthians 5:17[j], 1 John 1:8[k]). The battle of the new creation against the old nature becomes the defining battle in the Christian's life. Prayer, as the response of the faith of the new creation, cries out to God for the gifts that he has promised will keep us in the one true faith until death. Once we recognize how our old nature constantly fights against the new creation, Luther wrote, "we must find out where to get the [medicinal] herbs to enable us to live a good life and fulfil the commandments."[20] Luther's answer to this question is prayer.

The content of prayer for Luther is centered on the Christian's continual need for strength in the battle against the Devil, the world, and our sinful flesh, which would drive us away from faith. Luther's Small and Large Catechisms explain the Lord's Prayer in these terms. Luther says that God's will is done, according to the 3rd petition of the Prayer,

---

[i] And when the Lord smelled the pleasing aroma, the Lord said in his heart, "I will never again curse the ground because of man, for the intention of man's heart is evil from his youth. Neither will I ever again strike down every living creature as I have done. (Ge 8:21)

[j] Therefore, if anyone is in Christ, he is a new creation. The old has passed away; behold, the new has come. (2 Co 5:17)

[k] If we say we have no sin, we deceive ourselves, and the truth is not in us. (1 Jn 1:8)

> When God curbs and destroys every evil counsel and purpose of the devil, of the world, and of our flesh which would hinder us from hallowing his name and prevent the coming of his kingdom, and when he strengthens us and keeps us steadfast in his Word and in faith even to the end.[21]

Luther says that when we pray that God would deliver us from temptation, we are really praying that he would "guard and preserve us that the devil, the world, and our flesh may not deceive us or mislead us into unbelief, despair, and other great and shameful sins."[22] When we ask that God's kingdom might come, we are praying that "the heavenly Father gives us his Holy Spirit so that by his grace we may believe his holy Word and live a godly life, both here in time and hereafter forever."[23] The petitions of our prayers, according to Luther, should deal chiefly with our desire to persevere in the faith until we meet Christ face to face, either in this life or the next.

To truly know what to ask for in this regard, Luther says we must turn to the Scriptures and to the confessions of the Church. Time and again Luther uses the Ten Commandments, the Apostles' Creed, and the Lord's Prayer as guides for the devotional life of the Christian. These texts are faithful expositions of the Lord's Word, and as the speech of God to the Christian they show him the graciousness of his God, his own need for confession, the needs of his world for which he should petition God for help, and reasons for thanksgiving. In addition to the three chief parts of the Catechism mentioned above, Luther also found the psalms to be a useful guide for prayer. He suggested a number of psalms appropriate for meditation, including Psalms 10, 12, 20, 25, 51, 67, 79 and 103. Luther suggested a different subject of prayer for each psalm, such as a prayer against the Antichrist and his Kingdom (Psalm 10) and a prayer for the enemies of the Christian church and its gospel (Psalm 79). On the basis of the Psalms Luther urged prayer for the forgiveness of sins, the success of the Gospel, good government, and protection from Satan and his minions.

Although Luther is adamant that we should go to the Lord and no one else with all our concerns, he also warns that those concerns should flow out of God's revelation of his will for us. He speaks against, for example, asking God for signs, which he believes is a sign of unbelief on the part of the Christian. Likewise, when we pray for material needs, Luther stresses that our prayer should not be for those needs to be met as much as an expression of trust that God will indeed provide those needs. He writes that we should pray, "I would believe in God no less if I were poor, unintelligent, uneducated, despised, or lacking in everything."[24] This same thought is present in the Small Catechism, where Luther explains the fourth petition of the Lord's Prayer as a prayer that the Christian recognize God's provision of daily bread, which "he provides, even to the wicked, without our prayer."[25] "You see that we are praying here not for a crust of bread or for a temporal, perishable blessing, but for an eternal, priceless treasure and everything that God himself possesses."[26]

Furthermore, we ought not to come to God with answers to our prayers. God, as our true Father, knows our needs better than we ourselves (Matthew 6:32[1]). We can trust that our prayer will surely be granted, or something better than what we ask will be given in its stead. Luther also warns against "tempting" God by laying out the when, where and why of our prayer. In faith, we ought to trust that the Lord will certainly do the right thing in accordance with his unsearchable and divine wisdom.

---

[1] For the Gentiles seek after all these things, and your heavenly Father knows that you need them all. (Mt 6:32)

Prayer is not a matter of bringing concerns to God of which he was not previously aware. Prayer, instead, is an expression of trust that it is God, and God alone, who supplies our every need, helps us in every trouble, protects us from every danger, and is able to grant us eternal life. Scaer provides an excellent example of God answering our prayers in unanticipated ways.

> The man praying for chastity receives more temptations and the one praying for strength is besieged by more weaknesses. Nevertheless, as the Christian bears up under these stresses, God is answering the prayer more effectively than the man could ever have imagined.[27]

Prayer and "God For Us"

This leaves one last question to be addressed regarding Luther's understanding of prayer. It is often argued that if God is sovereign over all things, and foreknows and predestines all events, is there a point to petitionary prayer? Luther is aware of this question and addresses it in his writing regarding prayer for protection from the invading Turks.

> Beware of the Turkish, Epicurean philosophy which leads some to say, "What can I do? What is the use of praying? What does it help to worry? If it is predestined, it will happen." It is the belief of the Turks that no one may die unless his fated hour has come. That is the reason for their fanatical courage and their assurance that what they are doing is right. [28]

The answer to this question is in Luther's understanding of prayer as the response of faith. It is true that God is sovereign over all things; and yet God's sovereign will for creation is not accessible to either the unbeliever or the Christian. What the Christian does know is

God's will towards her; the Father, the Son and the Holy Spirit wish to give her all that they are and have. There is no good gift of faith, including forgiveness of sins, life and salvation, that God would hold back from those who have been brought to faith through the Gospel. Therefore God is sovereign, not in some abstract sense, but sovereign for us. Precisely because God is God for us is the question of God's predestinating of events irrelevant. God has called us to pray to him, to ask, to knock, to seek, and to trust: to reject this revealed will of God for us is in effect to abandon faith. We may intellectually believe in God, but we no longer trust that God. To quote C.S. Lewis, God said he would answer our prayers, "and he ought to know. We often talk as if He were not very good at theology!"[29] Luther himself writes much the same thing regarding the command to pray and its relation to God's predestining will. "We must be guided according to our calling, not according to that which we may think is predestined and about which we are in the dark and know nothing for certain."[30]

Conclusion

For Luther, prayer and faith go hand in hand. Faith receives the gifts of God, especially the Holy Spirit, who not only empowers our prayer back to God in return but also provides the very words of our prayer through the Scriptures and confessions of the church. In prayer we ask that our faith be strengthened, that we may be set to obey God's commandments and be strengthened in faith toward Jesus Christ. Our asking for the things of God is not a denial of God's sovereignty: the Lord remains God over all things. Yet we petition God in prayer because he has commanded us to do so, and has promised to hear us. Neither is our prayer a mere "whistling in the dark", or useless thing. Rather, our prayers reflect our faith that the God of the universe is also God pro nobis, giving to us all that he is and has. We pray in certainty that God, who has asked that we pray, given us the words to pray, and attached great promises to our prayer, will hear our prayers and gladly answer them as our dear heavenly Father. To this we add "amen - so be it."

> Finally, mark this, that you must always speak the Amen firmly. Never doubt that God in his mercy will surely hear you and say "yes" to your prayers. Never think that you are kneeling or standing alone, rather think that the whole of Christendom, all devout Christians, are standing there beside you and you are standing among them in a common, united petition which God cannot disdain. Do not leave your prayer without having said or thought, "Very well, God has heard my prayer; this I know as a certainty and a truth." That is what Amen means.[31]

---

[1] *Luther and Erasmus: Free Will and Salvation*. E. Gordon Rupp and Philip S. Watson, eds. (Philadelphia: The Westminster Press, 1969).

[2] Martin Luther, "The Bondage of the Will" in *Luther's Works, Vol. 33: Career of the Reformer III*, edited by Jaroslav Jan Pelikan, et. al. Luther's Works (Philadelphia: Fortress Press, 1999, c.1972). 139.

[3] Martin Luther, "Confession Concerning Christ's Supper" in *Luther's Works, Vol. 37: Word and Sacrament III*. Edited by Jaroslav Jan Pelikan, et. al. Luther's Works (Philadelphia: Fortress Press, 1999, c1972). 368.

[4] Martin Luther. "The Large Catechism" in *The Book of Concord: The Confessions of the Evangelical Lutheran Church*. Theodore Tappert, ed. (Philadelphia: Fortress Press, 2000, c1959). Para. 66.

[5] Philip Melanchthon. "The Apology to the Augsburg Confession" in *The Book of Concord: The Confessions of the Evangelical Lutheran Church*. Theodore Tappert, ed. (Philadelphia: Fortress Press, 2000, c1959). Article XXI, 10.

[6] David Scaer, "Luther on Prayer" in *Concordia Theological Quarterly* Vo. 47. No. 4. (October 1983). 306.

[7] Martin Luther. *What Luther Says: A Practical In-Home Anthology for the Active Christian*. Edwald Plass, ed. (Saint Louis: CPH, 1959). 1091.

[8] Melanchton, *Apology*, Article XII, 139.

[9] Melanchton, *Apology*, Article IV, 27.

[10] Martin Luther. "The Smalcald Articles" in *The Book of Concord: The Confessions of the Evangelical Lutheran Church*. Theodore Tappert, ed. (Philadelphia: Fortress Press, 2000, c1959). Article VIII, 8.

[11] Melanchton, *Apology*, Article XIII, 16.

[12] Martin Luther. "A Simple Way to Pray" in *Luther's Works, Vol. 43: Christian Devotion*, edited by Jaroslav Jan Pelikan, et. al. Luther's Works (Philadelphia: Fortress Press, 1999, c1972). 198.

[13] Martin Luther. "Personal Prayer Book" in *Luther's Works, Vol. 43: Christian Devotion*, edited by Jaroslav Jan Pelikan, et. al. Luther's Works (Philadelphia: Fortress Press, 1999, c1972). 11.

[14] Scaer, ibid, 305.

[15] Raymond Surburg, "The Biblical Means of Prayer", unpublished essay, 2.

[16] Martin Luther, "A Simple Way to Pray," 193.

[17] Jacques Ellul. *Prayer and the Modern Man.* (New York: Seabury Press, 1970). 111.

[18] Ellul, 125.

[19] Luther, "The Large Catechism," The Ten Commandments, 4.

[20] Luther, "Personal Prayer Book," 25.

[21] Martin Luther, "The Small Catechism," in *The Book of Concord: The Confessions of the Evangelical Lutheran Church.* Theodore Tappert, ed. (Philadelphia: Fortress Press, 2000, c1959). Para. 11.

[22] Luther, "The Small Catechism," The Lord's Prayer, 18.

[23] Luther, "The Small Catechism," The Lord's Prayer, 8.

[24] Luther, "Personal Prayer Book," 25.

[25] Luther, "The Small Catechism," The Lord's Prayer, 13.

[26] Luther, "The Large Catechism," The Lord's Prayer, 55.

[27] Martin Luther. "Appeal for Prayer Against the Turks" in *Luther's Works: Vol. 44: The Christian in Society I.* Edited by Pelikan, Jaroslav Jan, Hilton C. Oswald, and Helmut Lehmann. Luther's Works (Philadelphia: Fortress Press, 1999, c1972). 230.

[28] Luther, "An Appeal for Prayer Against the Turks," 235.

[29] Perry LeFevre. *Understandings of Prayer.* (Philadelphia: Westminster Press, 1981). 103.

[30] Luther, "An Appeal for Prayer Against the Turks," 236.

[31] Luther, "A Simple Way to Pray," 197.

Chapter 2: Prayer in the Age of Enlightenment

If one had to pick three theologians of the Enlightenment period whose thought can continue to be seen in contemporary theological understandings of prayer, they might well be Immanuel Kant, Freidrich Schleiermacher, and Karl Barth. Kant, with his theory of the categorical, or moral, imperative took religion out of the realm of dogmatic assertions and placed it squarely in the realm of ethics and morality. Schleiermacher, in reaction against both Kant's moral reductionism and the theology of the dogmaticians of his time, promoted a religion consisting solely of personal Gefühl, translated variously as feeling, consciousness, or awareness. Barth, in reaction against the kinds of theologies typified by Kant and Schleiermacher, sought a partial restoration of theology to the realm of confession, where one could once again make "dogmatic" assertions about the Christian God. Twentieth century understandings of prayer reflect, to a greater or lesser extent, either consciously or unconsciously, these three different approaches to religion, to God, and to the relationship between humanity and its Creator.

Immanuel Kant

Kant's greatest contribution to Christian thought was his shifting of religious activity out of the realm of the dogmatic and into the realm of the ethical. For Kant, God's essence and will are unknowable, since pure reason is unable to grasp the ding-an-sich - the thing in itself - of anything in the world, and certainly of God. Humans simply interpret the appearances of things around them that exist in time and space, which they then place into one of twelve different categories. God cannot, strictly speaking, be judged by his appearance. What we can know of God, for Kant, is roughly limited to what Deism can tell us about God: that he exists, that he created the universe, that he will punish good and reward evil in the next life.

True religion, for Kant, has little to do with worship of, or faith in, the God of Christian dogma.[1] Religion, instead, is concerned with ethics and the living of a moral life according to the moral "categorical imperative" all humans possess. For the Christian, this imperative may be shaped by Christ's ethical teachings, such as those contained in the Sermon on the Mount.

However, the teachings of Christ dealing with his salvific work, his person, or with prayer, need not necessarily be followed. For example, Kant says that prayer...

> ...is no more than a stated wish directed to a Being who needs no such information regarding the inner disposition of the wisher; therefore nothing is accomplished by it, and it discharges none of the duties to which, as commands of God, we are obligated; hence God is not really served.[2]

If God is omniscient, he already knows all things. To think of prayer, then, as an exchange of information with such a God is simply not reasonable. The concept of prayer as a response of faith seems to be excluded by Kant's understanding of faith itself. Kant describes faith as a "trust in God that he will supply our deficiency in things beyond our power, provided we have done all within our power."[3] Such a faith, however, would have little reason to resort to prayer: how can we ever be certain that we have done everything in our power? Would it not be presumptuous to ask God for his assistance when there may still be something we can do? Such an understanding of faith implies that we should trust God to help us only if we have first helped ourselves; otherwise, why look to God for help? This view, however, fits well with Kant's view of religion as being first and foremost an ethical obligation.

In Kant's thoughts on faith and religion is the beginning of a view
that will appear in later theologies of prayer. If religion is primarily
about ethics, and a sovereign God does not have need of nor desires
our words toward him, then prayer must be something that changes
us and helps us fulfill our moral obligations. A prayer life based on
such a theology would no longer flow out of faith in God. It would
instead flow out of the need to be guided in correct conduct. This is
the root of what will appear later as a Christian theology of prayer
abstracted from Christ and from faith.

Freidrich Schleiermacher

One of the greatest critics of Kant's neo-rationalist understanding of
religion, and Deist religion in general, was Freidrich Schleiermacher.
Raised by Moravian pietists, Schleiermacher had a profound respect
for the spiritual and the affective domain. He was gravely concerned
that spirituality was not just being removed from intellectual
discourse; it was in fact being removed from religion itself. Kant and
his followers were moving religion away from being a spiritual
encounter toward being a foundation for ethical behavior. At the
same time, scientific rationalism was making religion a mere sub-
branch of philosophy. To counter these moves, Schleiermacher
proposed that true religion was a tertium quid, being a part neither
of philosophy nor of ethics, but something independent from and
interacting with both.[4]

True religion, for Schleiermacher, is an awareness of absolute
dependence, and that God is the source of that dependence. It would
be a mistake to think, however, that Schleiermacher was returning to
religion a traditional Christian understanding of God. In fact, the
source of dependence that Schleiermacher calls "God" has no true
"personality" or "will" as Christians have traditionally attributed
those characteristics to God. Schleiermacher's God is "Highest Being,
not as personally thinking or willing, but exalted above all

personality, as the universal, productive, connecting necessity of all thought and existence."[5] "Whoever insists... that the highest piety consists in confessing that the Highest Being thinks as a person and wills outside the world, cannot be far traveled in the region of piety."[6] Certainly Schleiermacher's view of God is not much of an improvement on Kant's.

In what sense can we speak of prayer with such a Highest Being? For Schleiermacher, prayer must be understood in some other fashion than that of trying to bring about changes in God, or in God's attitude toward man, or in the world of persons and events. Schleiermacher believed that all human beings "anticipate, imagine, and hope in relation to the future, and combined with God- consciousness their thoughts become prayer."[7] Prayer is not a communication with the Highest Being, the Eternal, the All, of whichever other term Schleiermacher uses to represent that thing on which we are aware of being dependent. Prayer, rather, is the highest expectations of the religious person, the person who has become aware of their dependence on Something greater than themselves. In the case of the Christian religious person (and for Schleiermacher, one can be religious without being a Christian), that highest expectation is the realization of the Kingdom of God on earth. "Faith in the imperishable and supreme value of the Kingdom of God" must be the only kind of faith in which to pray.[8] Since awareness of the Kingdom of God is the point of religion for the Christian, prayer is the submission of our will to the One who wills that the Kingdom of God come: the Highest Being.[9] This view of prayer will also reappear in the 20th century among some popular theologians.

While Schleiermacher may have succeeded in restoring spirituality to religion, he ended up reinforcing Kant's depersonalization of God. The Deist God of Kantian philosophy is little distinguishable in attributes from Schleiermacher's Highest Being. In neither case is it possible to know God, at least in the sense that traditional Christian theology believed God could be known. In Kant's case, God cannot be known because God is not in a category accessible to pure reason. In Schleiermacher's case, God cannot be known because God does not possess the personal characteristics that would make him "knowable" as a being in any sense of the word. The only difference in their theologies is that Kant excludes the possibility of any kind of relation with God, while Schleiermacher insists that a relation of dependence with the Highest Being is the heart of religion. In both their cases, prayer no longer has God as an object, but the pray-er. For Kant, prayer has little value if God is sovereign and all things are present to him. One can only trust that God has under his control all those things that are beyond ours. In the meantime, one ought to be doing what one can, rather than praying for divine intervention. For Schleiermacher, prayer has value only in the sense that the pray-er brings his will into conformity with the will of the Eternal, Highest Being.

Karl Barth

Barth, the father of neo-orthodoxy, would be expected to provide a different understanding of prayer than both Schleiermacher and Kant. To a certain extent, this is the case. Barth rejected Kant's Deist, unknowable God, as well as Schleiermacher's Highest Being, as having departed so far from traditional Christian thinking as to be utterly incompatible with the Christian faith. Instead, Barth returned to the confessions of the Reformation and the Scriptures for his understanding of God, of faith, and of prayer. Himself of Reformed background, Barth leaned in the direction of Calvin and his followers rather than in that of Luther. He confessed that God was both sovereign and transcendent, but also that God had revealed himself in his Word. Outside of this Word, knowledge of God is impossible. But through the Word one encounters a gracious and merciful God, who desires to save people through participation in the Body of

Christ. This God is Wholly Other, who stands over and against humanity, and who challenges us with his Word. God comes to us in the proclamation of the Scriptures and not through our own consciousness, as Schleiermacher had proposed, or through our own human endeavors, as Kant had taught.[10]

Barth, therefore, grounded his theology of prayer in the Scriptural witness and the confessions of the Reformation, especially Luther's Small Catechism and the teachings of John Calvin. True prayer arises out of a confrontation with God's Word. In Barth's words, "I have heard his word, I wish sincerely to listen to it, and yet here I am in my insufficiency."[11] Prayer then arises out of the sense of the believer's own inadequacy and sin. More specifically, the Christian prays because God has commanded that he pray. More than that, God has promised to hear those prayers. "Doubt is permitted; even before we pray we must assume the attitude of a man who not has been heard."[12]

The greatest assurance we have that God hears even the most seemingly insignificant of our petitions is the incarnation. When God became man, "he interested himself in all these great things, and especially in all these small things, that preoccupy us."[13] These understandings of prayer seem to reflect Luther's own teaching regarding prayer, especially God's commanding it and his promises to hear it.

Where Barth departs slightly from Luther's understanding of prayer and bends closer to Calvin's perspective is on the content of prayer. Luther's prayer often centered on the request for protection from the temptations of sin, and the need for God to guard and protect us from the Devil, the world, and our sinful flesh which would lead us, not just into sinful behavior, but into false belief and despair. Calvin's emphasis was slightly different, in that his requests were for the leading of a righteous life before God. For example, in his explanation of second petition of the Lord's Prayer, Calvin writes, "God reigns where people, both by denial of themselves and by contempt of the world and of earthly life, pledge themselves to His righteousness in order to aspire to a heavenly life."[14]

Calvin also wrote that Christian pray "to testify and profess ourselves servants and children of God, zealously, truly, and deeply committed, to the best of our ability, to the honor that is owed our Lord and Father." He also urges Christians to pray God to "draw us back from worldly corruptions...kindle zeal for the mortification of the flesh."[15] This line of thinking is present throughout Calvin's explanation of the Lord's Prayer. In his understanding of prayer, Calvin assumes faith as a given, and is more concerned with the acts of the Christian life. We pray that God may lead us to be the sort of people he would have us be.

Contrast this with Luther, who writes that God's Kingdom comes "when the heavenly Father gives us his Holy Spirit so that by his grace we may believe his holy Word and live a godly life, both here in time and hereafter forever."[16] While both mention the need for a godly or heavenly life, Luther places the primary emphasis on the need for God alone to accomplish this, while Calvin, who would no doubt agree with Luther's explanation, implies the work of God, placing the emphasis on the description of the Christian life. Barth tends toward the latter. For example, Barth writes, "If we pray, 'Hallowed be thy name, thy kingdom come, thy will be done,' we place ourselves at God's side...God invites us to join his designs and his action."[17] This is not at all to imply any form of synergism in Barth's thought. Rather it serves to point out that he emphasizes prayer more as a companion to good works than as a request for forgiveness and protection from loss of faith.

Barth believes that prayer does exert an influence on God. This seems surprising for one with such a strong view of God's sovereignty. In fact, Barth states that it is precisely in yielding to our prayer that God shows his greatness. Therefore for Barth, unlike for Schleiermacher and Kant, petitionary prayer is not only effectual but commanded by God. Yet this view seems to be tempered by his understanding of how God answers prayer. Barth would agree, for example, with the statement that Christ - God becoming man - is the answer to all our prayers. He would also agree with the statement that all of our prayers have already been answered; again, because God has sent Christ and because Christ will return to reign. Therefore everything for which we pray is already accomplished in fact.

For Barth, then, prayer is commanded by God, and has the assurance that God will hear it. Both Calvin and Luther are agreed on this point. So Barth, to this extent, restores certain aspects of Luther's understanding of prayer for the 20th century. However Luther's understanding of prayer as the response of faith the Christian makes to the God who has saved him, continues to save him, and will save him in the end, is tempered somewhat. This view is replaced with Calvin's understanding of prayer as a request for help in living the Christian life rather than in preserving salvation.

Conclusion

The theological perspectives of Kant, Schleiermacher, and Barth on prayer will resurface again, whether explicitly in the case of more contemporary theologians or implicitly in the case of other writings on prayer. Parallels to Kant's neo-rationalism and reduction of religion to ethical behavior can be seen in the works of liberation theologians and other more radical theological figures. Echoes of Schleiermacher's theology will be present in the works of Evangelical writers who emphasize the personal awareness of a relationship with God. Barth's views, either on their own or as representative of modern thinking on Luther and Calvin, will be present in the works of more modern Lutheran and Reformed writers. Whether the authors acknowledge these men or merely reflect their understandings, all three represent to a certain extent the shape of the enlightenment period's theologies of prayer.

---

[1] Justo Gonzalez. *The Story of Christianity*. (Peabody, MA: Prince Press, 2001, c1984), 195.

[2] Perry LeFevre. *Understandings of Prayer*. (Philadelphia: Westminster Press, 1981), 11.

[3] LeFevre, 13.

[4] Frederich Schleiermacher. *On Religion: Speeches to Its Cultured Despisers.* John Oman, trans. (New York: Harper and Brothers, 1958, c1799), 20.

[5] Schleiermacher, 95.

[6] Schleiermacher, 99.

[7] LeFevre, 14.

[8] LeFevre, 15.

[9] LeFevre, 17.

[10] Gonzalez, 362.

[11] Karl Barth. *Prayer: According to the Catechisms of the Reformation.* (Philadelphia: Westminster Press, 1952), 20.

[12] Barth, 28.

[13] Barth, 40.

[14] John Calvin. *Writings on Pastoral Piety.* Elsie Ann McKee, ed. (New York: Paulist Press, 2001). 201.

[15] Calvin, 203.

[16] Martin Luther, "The Small Catechism," in *The Book of Concord: The Confessions of the Evangelical Lutheran Church.* Theodore Tappert, ed. (Philadelphia: Fortress Press, 2000, c1959). Lord's Prayer, 8.

[17] Barth, 38.

Chapter 3: Prayer in Contemporary Theology

The category of "contemporary theologian" could well describe any theological thinker of the late 20th century who has written on prayer. However, it is limited in this case to those who fall outside of the Lutheran tradition by their own understanding, as well as those outside of the Evangelical sub-culture of the United States. This category would include writers such as Karl Rahner, Paul Tillich, Thomas Merton, John A.T. Robinson, Dorothee Soelle, Simone Weil, and many others. It would include the subcategories of contemporary theology identified by Perry LeFevre as Liberation Theology, Secular Theology, Political Theology, Creation Theology and Linguistic Theology. Although all of these theologians approach both God and the subject of prayer in slightly different ways, there are commonalties that make presenting them as one category possible.

For example, there is a motif among all these theologians that prayer must be related to Christian action in the world. This is certainly true of Latin American Liberation Theologians such as Gustavo Gutierrez and Jan Sobrino, as well as Black, Feminist, and Womanist Theologians. But it is no less true for contemporary theologians that do not overtly belong to the tradition of the theology of liberation. In this sense Kant's religion of morality, usually implicitly rather than explicitly, continues to be present in our times. All of these theologians also share in a struggle over who, or what, God is. It is this struggle that underlies their reexamination of the purpose and content of prayer. In some of these writers, at least to a certain extent, echoes of Schleiermacher's religion of awareness are also present. But among these voices are also a few who dare to challenge the Zeitgeist of the times and look for an understanding of God and prayer more in line with ancient Christian confessions. This handful of discordant voices, to the extent that they are also "the new orthodox," is Barth's inheritance in the 20th century.

Representing these various points of view are the following four writers: Matthew Fox, C.S. Lewis, Jacques Ellul, and Roberta Bondi. Fox represents the view of prayer the most distant from traditional Christian confession, and is the one author most closely aligned with the views of Liberation Theologians. Lewis stands in for the modern apologists, interpreting ancient Christian views for the modern world. Lewis does not ignore contemporary theological developments, but instead engages them. French Reformed theologian Ellul takes a position similar to Lewis, although much closer to Reformation understandings of prayer and much more hostile to modern theological views. Bondi, a professor of church history at Emory University in Atlanta, has written a few books on prayer. She represents a unique position, in that she bases much of her understanding of prayer on the sayings of the Desert Fathers (and, in her words, Mothers) of the early church. Yet she filters her reading of those ancient writers through feminist eyes.

Matthew Fox

Matthew Fox is a former Roman Catholic priest who has written several books advocating a new approach to spirituality, including *Whee! We, Wee All The Way Home*, *The Coming of the Cosmic Christ*, and *On Becoming a Musical, Mystical Bear*. Despite their whimsical titles, Fox represents a very serious and profound form of Christian panentheism, which owes much to Schleiermacher's concept of religion as an awareness of the Eternal or the All. LeFevre calls Fox's theology "Creation Theology," in that it emphasizes God as creator and humans as his co- creators.[1]

Who is Fox's God?

God, for Matthew Fox, has an image problem; God will need to be re-imagined for a new generation if spirituality is to continue to be vibrant in western culture. "The difficulty in talking of God today is that the name, paraded for centuries as the Father of western culture, has lost it meaning within that falling culture."[2] Rather than the personal, transcendent, static God that Fox feels has dominated western civilization and Christianity, Fox seeks a return to a more Hebraic understanding of God as the Creator of a good creation and the giver of life, whose chief desire is that life be enjoyed by his creation. "God is the lover of life above all else; its preserver, its promiser, its enticer, its sharer."[3] This God must be recovered out of the depths of our selves. Awareness of God submerges the ego-consciousness of the human and replaces it with what Fox calls a "we-consciousness."[4] The God that emerges into our consciousness, which Fox sometimes calls "Providence," is an awareness of the One who is the Creator, the life-giver.

Fox finds this understanding of God as the one who underlies and grounds life to be, interestingly, rooted as much in the Old Testament as in the New Testament. He quotes, for example, Psalm 104:30[a], Job 12:10[b] and Genesis 1:2[c]. Fox also believes that this Life-giver can be understood as "Trinity," and attempts to retain some features of the biblical and confessional understanding of God. He sees the Holy Spirit as the one who is the life of the Father, given through the Son, present in us and in all creation. Fox identifies the Father with the one we find within ourselves who transforms our ego into a

---

[a] When you send forth your Spirit, they are created, and you renew the face of the ground. (Ps 104:30)

[b] He deprives of speech those who are trusted and takes away the discernment of the elders. (Job 12:20)

[c] The earth was without form and void, and darkness was over the face of the deep. And the Spirit of God was hovering over the face of the waters. (Ge 1:2)

collective consciousness. The Son, in turn, gives expression from within creation of God's will for humanity.[5]

God's relationship to humanity is not one of Righteous One to fallen creature, but one of Creator to creation, a creation called on to co-create alongside its Creator. Humans are called to be part of a creative, collective humanity. Sin, for Fox, is our fall into separateness and dualisms. Redemption is the restoration of humanity to wholeness, which comes through the life-giving Spirit of God. God's will is that we reject our separateness and become whole again. We are to be restored to the creative purpose of the image of God within us. Religion, in other words, "Worship, spirituality, (and) prayer need to be symbolized in a new way emphasizing horizontality, interdependence, shared ecstasies, justice."[6] This will only be accomplished, Fox believes, by returning to a Hebraic, rather than a Greek, way of thinking about the world and about God.

How Does Fox Understand Prayer?

Prayer, for Fox, is a radical response to life. Fox differentiates between a "reply" and a "response." A reply is an answer; a response is more. A response involves a commitment on the part of the responder. To respond to life, then, means to affirm life over and against its enemies. To say "Yes" to life is to say "No" to all that brings death: sexual, cultural, ideological and psychological exploitation of one group over another, which denies that wholeness of humanity. Fox identifies two aspects of prayer as a response to life. The first is the mystical, the identification of the "we" and the submerging of the "I". This mystical aspect of prayer is the pray-er's "Yes" to life and all that life entails. The second is prophetic, the commitment on the part of the pray-er to struggle against those who would say "No" to life. Because prayer is "inward - mystical, but also outward - prophetic, it functions not only to change the person, but also to change the world."[7]

How does one pray? How does one become mystical, finding God within and becoming a co- creator? How does one then, in turn, become prophetic, giving voice to the "we-consciousness" of which one has become aware? Fox spends much time identifying what he believes such prayer is not. It is not: saying prayers, withdrawal from one's culture, acquiescence to a culture, causing God to change by our petitions, talking to God, liturgy, or an exceptional experience. In contrast, Fox believes that prayer, at its core, is a meditation on life's mysteries: "Those moments that are recorded of Jesus in prayer are invariably provoked by real-life situations, by the very mysteries of life."[8] It is by meditating on these mysteries that the pray-er becomes aware of God and of his or her connection to all of creation. This awareness, in turn, leads one to an understanding of what one's prophetic voice in the world, against the enemies of life, must be. "If awareness is openness to the great in life, than among the great mysteries is ones own capacity for contribution to life: its birth and renewal, wrestling with its enemies."[9]

Prayer as Creative Awareness

For Fox, God is a "we-awareness" that causes the individual to transcend her own point of view and see herself as part of all creation. In this sense, Fox's theological approach to prayer is not qualitatively different from Schleiermacher's "religion-as-awareness" theology. However, Fox adds to this theology a deep appreciation for God as the Creator, the one who gives life to all that is. This Creator is not so much over and against creation, as part and parcel of it, so much so that Fox can identify "response to life" and "response to God" as being essentially the same thing. Fox, in this regard, is a panentheist, believing not that all created things are gods, but rather that God is immediately present in all of creation, and nowhere else. Prayer, then, is no longer language spoken to a personal Creator in whom one has "faith" or "trust," but time spent reflecting on life in order to come to a deeper appreciation of one's own place in it and responsibilities towards it.

Jacques Ellul

"To raise the problem of prayer is to raise the problem of faith in the contemporary world."[10] So writes Jacques Ellul, the French Reformed theologian and ethicist of the late twentieth century. Ellul is perhaps best known for his challenge of the western world's obsession with "technique," defined by Ellul as the unquestioned belief that scientific and technological advances are of intrinsic worth. Less known, perhaps, are Ellul's theological works, including *The Subversion of Christianity* and *Prayer and Modern Man*. These books take aim at enlightenment and modern liberal theological thinking, confronting them using fresh and contemporary presentations of classic Reformation thought. In *Prayer and Modern Man*, Ellul uses some of the basic Reformation ideas regarding prayer, especially prayer as faithful obedience to God's command, to challenge contemporary theological positions on the subject.

Who is Ellul's God?

Ellul does not hide his loathing of modern theological perspectives on God. He mocks views of God that make him neither substantive nor substance, or which rename God as the Ultimate, as Depth, as Structure, the creating ground of our existence, the goal of our social life, the source of our historical existence. Such definitions, Ellul writes, are "entirely abstract - more so than the dogmas of the Trinity."[11] Not only are these definitions of God faulty, they are also detrimental and antithetical to the Christian faith. "That 'little candle stub which is still smoldering' - theology carefully extinguishes it."[12] In the place of such abstract concepts of God, Ellul promotes classic Trinitarian theology. The God to whom we pray is not some unknown quantity, but "The God who is incarnate in the human condition, who empties himself, who dies, because he loves man."[13] To no other God is prayer truly possible.

To demonstrate that this is so, Ellul shows the connection between modern views of God and modern perspectives on prayer. Since God is no longer viewed as a personal, transcendent deity who is wholly other than us, and against whom we are in rebellion, the locus of prayer has shifted from God to the pray-er. Ellul levels a strong indictment against this shift, seeing in it the worst form of self-idolatry:

> With what seeming humility do we in fact divert prayer hypocritically from its truth in which God is at the center, in order to put ourselves once again at the center of the operation. Thus to pretend that God is too great is a subtle way of recovering the principle role for ourselves.[14]

Under the guise of preserving the sovereignty of the "Ground of All Being," modern theologians have made man, rather than God, the object of prayer. Modern theologians, in Ellul's opinion, have developed "a theology of justification which takes a cheap view of prayer and also of the Fatherhood of God. The two go together."[15] For Ellul, the one who prays truly is the one who knows God truly. Such a one knows in what he hopes. He knows in whom he believes. Only such knowledge can open up the possibility of true prayer.

True theology - words about God - is absolutely necessary for prayer. Christian theology teaches, first of all, that it is God that makes prayer possible. God renders prayer possible, first of all, by the work of the Holy Spirit. The Holy Spirit does not merely help prayer - he is the one who actually prays in and for us. Ellul interprets Romans 8:26-27 in keeping with this line of thinking. This phrase, in his opinion, has too often been interpreted as though the Holy Spirit added a little something to our prayers. This view suggests that "our prayer is incomplete, unsatisfactory... That is quite incorrect. It is the entire prayer which is the prayer of the Holy Spirit."[16] Our prayers are not our own, but the work of the Holy Spirit in us. If we do not understand this intimate involvement of God in our prayer, we do understand what is occurring in prayer.

Ellul also quotes Pascal's *Pensées* as an appropriate understanding of prayer in relation to the sovereign will of God. God grants us prayer for three reasons, according to Pascal. The first is to give to his creatures the "dignity of causality:" by our prayer, we converse with he who is the first cause, and participate in his activity in the world. We are not left out of God's sovereign will for the world, but included in it through prayer, which God promises to hear. The second reason for prayer is to teach us about God and how we obtain virtue from him. Pascal, a Jansenist, understood the corruption of the human nature and the need for God to turn the will from evil toward good. Ellul, a Reformed Christian, understands this as well. He sees the corruption of man as one of the reasons why prayer is so necessary. He quotes Rousseau's *Émile* as a counter- example of why recognition of our sinful condition is so necessary for prayer:

> What am I to ask (God) for? All I ask of him is the ability to do good. Why ask him for what he has given me? Has he not given me a conscience for loving the good, my reason to enable me to know it, freedom to do it? To ask him to change my will⬚is to want him to do my work.[17]

Ellul's response to Rousseau's rhetorical question is this: "I must realize that if I pray I signify that I am inclined to evil."[18] We do not have the ability to do good, apart from God, and that is why we must pray.

How Does Ellul Understand Prayer?

For Ellul, the idea that prayer can be reduced to works of charity toward our neighbor is one of the deepest errors of modern liberal theologians. It once again places man and his actions at the center of prayer, rather than God. "...That dreadful motto, 'To work is to pray,' dreadful because of the cynicism, the justification, the contempt which it expresses... (it) justifies oneself before men (how could it be before God?)"[19] Prayer must be speech toward God. But how can one understand this speech, if the modern ideas of prayer as God-consciousness, morality, or co- creation with God are merely forms of human self-justification? Ellul sees the true basis for prayer in God's command that we ask him for those things of which we have need. 'Watch and pray' - that is the sole reason for praying which remains for modern man. No other enticement to prayer will work, and no other reason for prayer is faithful to the God revealed in the Scriptures.

We pray because God has commanded us to pray. This command of God to pray, however, should not be regarded as Law, but as "Gospel imperative." Ellul writes, "What is understood in the commandment is a promise..."[20] The command to pray entails, first of all, a promise that prayer as conversation toward God is really possible and second, that the door will be opened for us. If all this is so, then prayer must be related to faith. Without faith, how can one believe the promises that God has attached to prayer? Ellul sees faith and prayer as inseparably connected. "The first expression of faith is prayer."[21] But since faith is a work of the Holy Spirit, God must be the one motivating prayer. Faith in God must precede prayer, which is the response to the command of the God who has brought us to faith. So Ellul can write, "Prayer is never other than... a response to the word of invitation first made known in the Scripture."[22]

What should be the content of our prayer? Since in coming to God in prayer we recognize our own sinfulness, prayer must first of all be a desire to be kept in faith. "We have to continue to pray because on that prayer depends the maintaining of faith."[23] To be kept in faith means that God shapes our will into conformity with his, so that our prayer that his will be done is not hypocrisy or indifference. Not hypocrisy, in that God has created in us a desire to see his will done, and not indifference, in that we know what God's will is: our salvation. A prayer of any other kind cannot be in conformity with God's will. Selfish desires are necessarily excluded from proper prayer, for selfishness is never in conformity with God's will. Our understanding of God's will comes from the Scriptures, especially Christ's own prayers. Ellul writes, "The model furnished by Jesus is the anti-consumer prayer par excellence."[24]

Prayer as the Response to Divine Command

God, for Ellul, is the Father who sent his Son into the world out of his great love for us, and brings us to faith in his saving work through the Holy Spirit. We pray to this God, who has revealed himself to us, that he might preserve our faith and bring our will into conformity with his. Ellul grounds the object and content of prayer on the command of God in Scripture. God has told us to pray, and has promised to hear us. Who are we to contradict him? Furthermore, God has provided the content of our prayers through Christ's own prayers. We know, then, for what we should pray. Petitionary prayer is not useless, even in the face of a Sovereign God, for God desires that we participate in his actions through our prayers. Ellul encourages prayer by paraphrasing a story from the ministry of the Lord: "Launch out into the deep and cast your net. You do not know it, but the fish are there waiting for you, even though all night they were not there. Launch out!"[25]

Roberta Bondi

Roberta Bondi has written a few books on prayer, including *To Pray and To Love, A Place to Pray,* and *Memories of God.* In *Memories of God* she recounts how she found a place for herself as a women in what she felt was a patriarchal religion through reading the works of the desert fathers and mothers of the early church.[26] As a result, her view of God is not antithetical to traditional Christian confessions, although her emphases sometimes differ from them, and also from the teachings of the early church writers who guide most of her thought.

Who is Bondi's God?

For Bondi, God is first, foremost, and above all else, love. God is a God of "wild grace, who delights in us, who for tender love for us in Jesus Christ has taken on all the darkness, pain, ambiguity, and vulnerability of what it means to be a human being."[27] She believes that the early church taught that "God's love for us as human beings precedes, enables, and gives meaning to all human love and prayer."[28] Far from seeing God's love as "the cold winter wind that bites and penetrates and shakes and testifies" of Pseudo-Dionysius the Aeropagite,[29] Bondi sees God's love as the embrace of a parent who wants only the best for his or her children. Christ is the fullest expression of this love, and is God's pledge to us that his love is without end or limit.

This does not mean, however, that God's love is without any shape or form. God's love is not mere emotion or feeling, but is an expression of his desire for a fulfilling life for all his creatures. God desires that we show love and compassion toward ourselves and toward each other. Bondi interprets God's judging activity as the disciplining work of a parent:

> Christians who live with an ongoing sense of the love,
> goodness, and generosity of God often find it hard to find a
> way of reconciling that love with any talk of God's
> judgment... But judgment means something quite different if
> we seek God's friendship and wish to live in it... judgment is
> an act of God's friendship toward us as God daily holds us
> accountable to the friendship.[30]

God's judgment, then, is not to be feared, but to be embraced as his
loving work. God's work in Christ is not to be seen as a satisfaction
for sin, but instead as a pledge of the love God has always shown
toward us, as well as an example of how we too should live. To deny
this view, and become preoccupied with our status as sinful human
beings, is detrimental to prayer. Bondi writes that, "such a conviction
encourages us to think and feel that although we have an assurance
of God's love for us displayed in Christ, we should never approach
God without an awareness of our sinfulness and unworthiness."[31]
Bondi's view of God, then, tends to be the God of social democracy:
God is love, is compassionate towards all people, desires that we
care and love for each other, and disciplines us (gently) when we do
not.

Bondi retains the possibility of communication with God. He is not so
transcendent or impersonal that language with him is meaningless.
Neither is speech with God in prayer "useless," in the sense of having
no effect on an immutable God. In fact, Bondi sees in Jesus' encounter
with the Canaanite woman proof that the will of God can indeed be
changed through prayer. However this does not mean that God's
actions will necessarily always be changed to suit our needs. God's
will is that we trust that his decisions are best. "We hope to receive
what we ask for, but we also accept that when we pray, we never
know what the outcome of our prayer will be."[32] God's will is also
that we ask in prayer for those things he already desires for us and

for others. "Whenever we long for and pray for the well being of other people, we are only asking God for what God already longs for more than we."[33]

How Does Bondi Understand Prayer?

Bondi believes that the root of all prayer is the desire for God. She believes firmly that in prayer, as in life, we are to seek our true identify in God as his children. Our identity cannot be found in the things of this world, but only in him. Prayer is the answer to the question, "Who am I, and what am I doing here?" Human beings need love and relationality to live; only God can provide the love and relationality that we seek. So for Bondi, prayer is intimately linked with our friendship with God, and our friendship toward all humanity. To pray is to build those relationships and seek to improve them.

Bondi can therefore say that true prayer is more than just saying prayers. It is also "Thinking and reflecting, pondering what it would mean to love specific people in our lives..." and "The development and practice of loving ways of being."[34]

Bondi roots this understanding of prayer in the teachings of the monastics of the early church. "For the monastics, the work of prayer is never separated from growth in the patterns of love..."[35] These patterns of love are humility, discernment, consultation, and acknowledgement of sin. By acknowledgment of sin Bondi does not mean an acknowledgment of a broken relationship with God, but rather actions that display our lack of genuine love toward God and toward one another. "Only a small part of our prayer, however, is sitting down every day and deliberately spending time with God as we read Scripture, listening to God's voice, trying to make sense of our lives in God's presence, and praying for others."[36]

The other part of prayer involves doing love in the world. If prayer is friendship with the God who loves us, Bondi believes we should pray for the same things God wants. "Friends want the same things. According to Theodoret, 'this is the definition of friendship: liking and hating the same things.' What is it that we should like and hate, that God likes and hates? God's deepest desires are for the healing and well-being of all creation."[37] Our prayers, then, are centered on our desire to display a God-like attitude toward our fellow human beings, and indeed, toward all creation. There are several places we can go in order to better understand God's will and bring our attitude in line with his. First, there are the Scriptures. Bondi believes the psalms are an especially valuable place to start prayer. Yet the Scriptures are only one way that God shares himself with us. Spending silent time with God in "centering prayer" can also be valuable.

Prayer as an Act of Love and Friendship

Bondi builds her understanding of prayer on her belief that friendship with a loving, caring and compassionate God, who wants abundant life for all people, is the center of Christianity. She draws much of her insight from the early church monastics. However, it is worth noting what she overlooks in the early church's understanding of prayer. Most of the early church fathers understood the value and effect of prayer to be intimately tied up with the moral behavior of the pray-er. Cyprian wrote, "Prayer is ineffectual when the petition offered to God is sterile... Quickly do those prayers ascend to God which the merits of our works urge upon him."[38] Origen reconciled God's sovereignty with petitionary prayer by writing "God foresees those prayers that will merit satisfaction and prearranges the created order to that end."[39] By downplaying, or perhaps overlooking, this aspect of the early church fathers' theology of prayer, Bondi gives a false impression of the true theology of the monastics. Certainly they believed in a God of love, and of his love toward humanity. But one cannot understand their writings on prayer without also understanding how their views were tied up with the necessity to live a pure, virtuous life. For the early monastics, the judgment of God was not gentle correction, but a very present and harsh reality. However, Bondi seems to have correctly interpreted the monastics' view that prayer is wrapped up in our actions. One cannot profess to love God and hate one's brother (1 John 4:20[d]). "Prayer is hypocrisy is a man's life does not exemplify his aspiration in prayer."[40] One might summarize Bondi's view of prayer this way: God is love; in prayer we accept his love and friendship, and learn to love our world as God loves it.

C.S. Lewis

C.S. Lewis was a professor at Cambridge University, in addition to being a well-known lay theologian in the Church of England. Lewis wrote several books that touched on the idea of prayer, most importantly his Letters to Malcolm. Although not averse to considering non- traditional views on such subjects as the resurrection of the body, for the most part Lewis remained committed to Orthodox Christianity, including an insistence on belief in the supernatural as an important part of faith. Likewise his understanding of prayer, while in some places providing new insight, tends to be traditional.

Who is Lewis' God?

Lewis' understanding of God seems to be, to a great extent, the God of natural reason. Lewis does not make direct reference to the Trinity. Neither does he directly apply the dogma of the Trinity to prayer. God is God, and that's that. God, for Lewis, is both transcendent and immanent. One cannot, and should not, think of God as close without also thinking of him as other. "We ought to be,"

---

[d] If anyone says, "I love God," and hates his brother, he is a liar; for he who does not love his brother whom he has seen cannot love God whom he has not seen. (1 Jn 4:20)

Lewis writes, "simultaneously aware of closest proximity and infinite distance."[41] The Christian must be forever on guard against turning God into some impersonal "ground of being," or of thinking of him as so transcendent that he can have no relationship with his creation. Lewis puts it this way: "When one is among Pantheists one must emphasize the distinctnessof the creatures. Among Deists one must emphasize the divine presence in my neighbor, my dog, my cabbage patch."[42]

The concept of a God of justice - of wrath - as well as a God of mercy and good news is very much present in Lewis' thought. Sin cannot simply be argued away. In fact, Lewis writes, "All the liberalizing and "civilizing" analogies only lead us astray. Turn God's wrath into mere enlightened disapproval, and you also turn His love into mere humanitarianism."[43] To destroy the Law is to make the Gospel of Jesus Christ meaningless and trite. To put it another way, if there is no evil, then what sense ought we make of the requirement to love one's neighbor? If we love our neighbor by nature, there would be no need for such a command.

The attributes one normally associates with God - his omniscience, omnipotence, and omnipresence - are all affirmed by Lewis. God's sovereignty over all creation and its creatures is likewise acknowledged. Given his tendency to approach theology from a philosophical point of view, how does Lewis then understand God's actions in relation to our prayers? Lewis acknowledges the difficulty in reconciling making requests of God who already knows and causes all things:

> Is it our faith that prayers, or some prayers, are real causes? But they are not magical causes: they don't, like spells, act directly on nature. They act, then, on nature through God? This would seem to imply that they act on God. But God, we

believe, is impassible. All theology would reject the idea of a transaction in which a creature was the agent and God the patient.[44]

How Does Lewis Understand Prayer?

Lewis will not grant that petitionary prayer is therefore worthless. God does indeed act on and answer our prayer. He grounds his belief that petitionary prayer is of value in God's forgiveness. "If he takes our sins into account, why not our petitions?"[45] Lewis finds his solution in God's eternal foreknowledge. Just as God "chose us in him before the foundation of the world," (Ephesians 1:4) so too did he take into account our prayers. "If our prayers are granted at all, they are granted from the foundation of the world."[46] Whether or not they are granted is actually not the most important thing. What is important is that God hears all our prayers and includes them in his plan of action. "But really, for our spiritual life as a whole, the 'being taken into account,' or 'considered,' matters more than the being granted."[47] Lewis sums up his understanding of the relationship between God's sovereign will and our petitions this way:

> But how can (prayer) change God's will? Well - but how very odd it would be if God in his actions toward me were bound to ignore what I did (including my prayers). Surely he hasn't to forgive me for sins I didn't commit... In other words his will... must be related to what I am and do. And once grant that, and why should my asking or not asking not be one of he things He takes into account? At any rate He said he would - and He ought to know.[48]

God desires to know us. This knowledge of us is more than mere knowledge about us. Lewis believes that God knows everything about us in his omniscience, but what he truly desires is to know us in the "biblical" sense. Prayer, then, is a means by which we open ourselves up to relationship - to being known - by God. "Instead of merely being known, we show, we tell, we offer ourselves to view."[49] So beyond petitioning God in prayer, we also open ourselves up to him in trust. Our prayer life should be such that one goes to God with every concern and thought, never limiting our words, as we would to a parent who asks about the events of the day.

Prayer should also the one who prays outside of himself and toward God and neighbor. God has called us to love him and to love our neighbor; we already have quite enough love of self to go around. Lewis writes,

> Prayer itself is this movement out from the self and is part of the basic pattern of salvation and sanctification which involves the loss of self to gain the self...That is why prayer should relate to real people, real actions in the world, rather than toward the cultivation of the inner spirit... [50]

Prayer as Relationship with God

Lewis understands God as one who is both transcendent and immanent, who desires to know us, have a relationship with us, and have our trust - our faith. By praying, we open ourselves to a relationship with God. God has already taken our prayers into account from the beginning of the world, and this should motivate us to make our requests known before him. The content of our prayers should be both our daily needs and wants, from the small and mundane to the great and important, as well as petitions for others in our world. Prayer should not turn us inward toward self, but outward.

Conclusion

Bondi, Fox, Ellul and Lewis all share a belief in the importance of prayer. All of them believe that prayer, in some sense, should involve

God. There, however, the similarities end. Fox's theology of prayer tends in the same direction as Schleiermacher's, seeing God as an awareness of the root of all life, and as Kant's, seeing religion as concerned with moral action. Lewis' God, while possessing many of the attributes familiar to western theologians, lacks a strong Trinitarian focus, and so ends up being similar to the God of Schleiermacher in the sense of being better named "The Eternal" than "The Father, the Son and the Holy Spirit." Likewise Bondi's God seems to contain more projections of attributes onto God than the early church would have likely found acceptable. Although she does speak of God as Triune, the Son's atoning work is downplayed to such an extent that either the Father or the Holy Spirit could have become incarnate with much the same effect. Only Ellul focuses at some length on God's Trinitarian nature, and especially on the importance of the Incarnation for our relationship with the Father and the possibility of prayer. In this sense, Ellul is following in the footsteps of Barth's attacks on liberal theology, favoring a return to a more traditional understanding of the Godhead.

All the writers include in their theology of prayer an understanding of prayer as relating to others and to the world. Even Fox, who emphasizes more than the others the mystical nature of prayer, also speaks of prayer as prophetic and focusing outward on the world. Bondi, like Fox, speaks of prayer as including one's actions towards one's neighbors in the world. Ellul and Lewis include the neighbor in their theology of prayer as one who should be brought before God. Certainly all four believe that lack of love for one's neighbor is incongruous with prayer life. Ellul, Bondi and Lewis all believe in the value of petitionary prayer. For Bondi, however, our petitions should center more on ourselves and our need to change. Lewis and Ellul are bolder in their assertion that God indeed desires our petitions and acts on them. Both use a similar line of argumentation that God takes or is already taking our petitions into account. Ellul emphasizes God's graciousness is allowing us to participate in his actions, while Lewis is more interested in explaining this from an intellectual and philosophical point of view. Of the four authors, Ellul is the closest to Luther's understanding of prayer as the trusting response of the Christian to God's promises. This theme also appears to a certain extent in Lewis. Bondi is more concerned about how prayer might conform us to God's will, as is Fox. In the end, one can say that contemporary theologians lack a strong sense of humans as sinners, and as God as Redeemer. They therefore see prayer in ways other than as a radical trust in the One who is able and willing to save.

---

[1] Perry LeFevre. *Radical Prayer: Contemporary Interpretations.* (Chicago: Exploration Press, 1982), i.

[2] Matthew Fox. *On Becoming a Musical, Mystical Bear.* (Mahwah, NJ: Paulist Press and Deus Press, 1976), 60.

[3] Fox, 62.

[4] LeFevre, 51.

[5] Fox, 154.

[6] LeFevre, 55.

[7] LeFevre, 50.

[8] Fox, 58.

[9] Fox. 81.

[10] Jacques Ellul. *Prayer and the Modern Man.* C. Edward Hopkins, trans. (New York: Seabury Press, 1970).

[11] Ellul. 94.

[12] Ellul, 98.

[13] Ellul, 112.

[14] Ellul, 26.

[15] Ellul, 90.

[16] Ellul, 62.

[17] Ellul, 80.

[18] Ellul, 81.

[19] Ellul, 15.

[20] Ellul, 104.

[21] Ellul, 116.

[22] Ellul, 123.

[23] Ellul, 108.

[24] Ellul, 146.

[25] Ellul, 128.

[26] Roberta Bondi. *Memories of God.* (New York: Abingdon Press, 1995).

[27] Roberta Bondi. *To Pray and to Love: Conversations on Prayer with the Early Church.* (Minneapolis: Fortress Press, 1991), 137.

[28] Bondi, *To Pray and to Love,* 126

[29] Jeffrey Burton Russell. *The Prince of Darkness*. (Ithaca: Cornell University Press, 1988).
[30] Bondi, *To Pray and to Love*, 126.
[31] Bondi, *To Pray and to Love*, 135.
[32] Bondi, *To Pray and to Love*, 131.
[33] Bondi, *To Pray and to Love*, 132.
[34] Bondi, *To Pray and to Love*, 14.
[35] Bondi, *To Pray and to Love*, 100.
[36] Bondi, *To Pray and to Love*, 13.
[37] Bondi, *To Pray and to Love*, 123.
[38] Robert L. Simpson. *The Interpretation of Prayer in the Early Church*. (Philadelphia: Westminster Press, 1965), 126.
[39] Simpson, 123.
[40] Simpson, 131.
[41] C. S. Lewis. *Letters to Malcolm: Chiefly on Prayer*. (San Diego: Harvest Books, 1992, c1964), 13.
[42] Lewis, 74.
[43] Lewis, 97.
[44] Lewis, 48.
[45] Lewis, 50.
[46] Lewis, 48.
[47] Lewis, 52.
[48] LeFevre, 103.
[49] Lewis, 21.
[50] LeFevre, 107.

Chapter 4: Prayer and American Evangelicals

Author Lee Strobel writes in his preface to the book, *The Prayer of Jesus*, that there are over 8,202 books on prayer listed on the Amazon.com website. That number has now swelled. Certainly there is no lack of books on the subject of prayer. Some of the most prolific writers of "how-to" books on prayer are found in what has been identified by one author as the "Evangelical sub-culture." The titles of these books invariably promise solutions to the dry or empty prayer lives of Christians based on the author's insights into God's will or revelation in Scripture. The dustcovers of several of these books serve as an example (emphasis the author's)

> As God unfolded His plan for her life, she began to understand what it meant to live in God's will. And she found that she could share her discovery with other people.[1]

> Discover how the remarkable prayer of a little known Bible hero can release God's favor, power and protection.[2]

> (This) is not a comfortable book to read. It makes you look at your own habits and thoughts. But it will also offer some startling insights on the power of personal prayer.[3]

The writers of these prayer books, all of which are examined in this chapter, share in common a desire to "kick their readers' Christian lives into high gear." The one author who appeared the least bit critical to this approach still succumbed to their technique. The cover of his book promoted its content with the words, "The prayer of Jesus revolutionized (the disciples) lives. It can revolutionize yours as well!"[4]

The five authors chosen as representative of this tradition were picked not so much for the quantity of their writings on prayer as for their prominence within the Evangelical sub-culture. Bill Gothard, for example, is well known to D. James Kennedy, the prominent televangelist from Coral Ridge Presbyterian Church in Florida, as well as to Bruce Wilkinson, now famous for his own book on prayer, *The Prayer of Jabez*. This latter book was also included, if only for its unparalleled popularity and widespread availability. Bill Hybels' book on prayer was included because of his prominence as the senior preacher of the Willow Creek Community in Illinois, acknowledged as one of the largest congregations of Christians in the United States, and the home church of a unique and widely used church planting methodology. Hank Hanegraaff is also a prominent figure in the Evangelical community, as the president of the Christian Research Institute and the host of the "Bible Answer Man" broadcast. Stormie Omartian, while not as well known a figure, has written numerous books on prayer, including a series of books beginning with *The Power of a Praying Woman*.

Bill Gothard

Bill Gothard is the President and Founder of the Institute in Basic Life Principles. The institution has as its stated aim "training young people to be mighty in spirit, mature in character, and wise in decision-making according to biblical truth."[5] His book on prayer, The Power of Crying Out, has received praise from significant and influential segments of the Evangelical community. Such notables as Charles Stanley (radio and television preacher), Bill Bright (founder of Campus Crusade for Christ), Pat Boone, and Bruce Wilkinson (author of *The Prayer of Jabez*) all praise this short, ninety-one page book. D. James Kennedy, the author of Evangelism Explosion writes, "Bill Gothard is synonymous with rapier-like penetration of every aspect of the dedicated Christian life... Bill Gothard's anecdotal approach to the kind of prayer that gets real answers from God

makes for lively and rewarding reading." Further tying together this
small community of writers is Gothard's footnote on page 94 of his
book, "Be sure to read Dr. Bruce Wilkinson's life-changing book, The
Prayer of Jabez."

Who is Gothard's God?

Gothard believes that God wants to demonstrate "His loving care and
His powerful hand of protection" to all believers in Christ. God is
certainly omnipotent, omniscient, and omnipresent, able and willing
to answer the requests of his children. He is most particularly
interest in bestowing blessing, a theme which appears in much of the
Evangelical literature. Although blessing is never identified crassly
with material goods or even earthly prosperity, it certainly enables
one to get more out of the Christian life than would otherwise be
possible. When prayers are effective, God will work powerfully to
save lives, help Christian institutes acquire needed property, and
grant numerical blessings to evangelism work. For Gothard, "God's
ultimate purpose in all creation is to demonstrate His glory." This
glory consists in the Lord's "work in our lives, and also... the Lord's
gospel (his greatest work!)."[6] God is also the source of our prayers.
"The Holy Spirit Himself is at work within us to prompt our crying
out aloud to God. And because God is compassionate, gracious, and
always faithful to His promise, He will indeed hear and answer these
cries that He Himself inspires."[7] Beyond this, Gothard has little to say
about the nature of God himself.

How Does Gothard Understand Prayer?

God, first of all, requires and expects us to pray. God looks for us to
call on him in times of trouble, and expect help only from him. We
should pray "boldly expecting his deliverance. God invites and
expects His beloved ones to do exactly that."[8] This is especially true
when we're confronted with God's law, and realize how much we
have fallen short of it. "We cry out for the Lord's help when we
realize that what's required of us is vastly beyond our abilities."[9] But

the prayer of confession, for Gothard, is necessary only to prepare us for true prayer. God desires to work powerfully in our lives, removing worldly obstacles, and demonstrating to the world, through us, his glory. The word Evangelicals - Gothard among them - associate with this demonstration of God's glory is blessing. God desires to bestow blessings on us. Blessings usually refer to contentment, peace of mind, joy, and a general feeling of well being. The better the prayer, the more likely God is to answer it with blessing: which, of course, God wants to do. "Surely this greater blessing can also be ours as we meditate with the same demonstrated intensity - just like the heightened blessing that can accompany spoken prayer."[10]

The chief way to improve the quality of our prayer, and the likelihood of it being effective, is by praying out loud. God desires that we pray out loud and not merely silently in our hearts. "God hears our prayers... He particularly hears us when our requests are voiced aloud."[11] This core insight was the impetus behind the book, and the reason for the title, *The Power of Crying Out*. Gothard believes this principle of praying out loud is a biblical principle present in both the Old and New Testaments. "I saw that the Bible itself makes a distinction between 'prayer' and 'crying out to God.'"[12] Gothard recounts this story at the end of the book to make his point about crying out to God:

> But maybe you've also begun to feel a little empty sometimes... as if God was very distant and far away from you... and you've begun to wonder if He's hearing your prayers at all. A friend of mine recently described his own experience with giving loud voice to prayers... His doubts kept telling him that is was 'just a gimmick'... but he began to do it anyway. Immediately, something happened. Tears sprang to his eyes.[13]

Prayer, for Gothard as well as other Evangelicals, takes on a sacramental character. It takes the place of baptism, in a sense, by being the means of transition from the world to the kingdom of God. Gothard himself believes that "Those who genuinely cry out to the Lord for salvation are instantly born again by the Spirit God, who then dwells forever within them and energizes of them to cry out for further needs."[14] The crying aloud of the petitioner in prayer is a regenerative means of grace. This does not mean, however, that true and sincere faith is not a prerequisite for prayer. For example, Gothard also believes that doubts can get in the way of our prayers being heard. He quotes Charles Spurgeon in this regard, who said, "He who prays without fervency does not pray at all." He goes on to say, "Much of our prayer lacks the kind of fervency God requires for effective results."[15] This then puts him in a corner: how do we deal with a lack of fervency in prayer? What do we do if we feel our prayers are not sincere enough? In this case, we must confess our doubt to God in prayer, "ask God to remove it, and cry out again in faith."[16]

Effective prayer is the prerequisite to God working in our life. Without prayer, God cannot lift so much as a divine finger to help us out. Gothard says that God "will arrange or allow circumstances to arise that seem to have no solution... until I cry out. And not one second sooner!"[17] He also writes, "Only when we cry out to Him in desperation does He calm the storms in our lives."[18] Our prayers should be out loud, and they should be made in sincerity and trust in God's promise to answer. The best way to do the latter is to do the former. Prayer is also linked with obedience to God in other areas of our life. "Our true, absolute surrender will include obedience to God's command to be His loving ambassadors in humble service to those around us, especially those in great need."[19]

Crying Out in Prayer

For Gothard, the life of the Christian is one of blessing and victory over Satan. If only our prayers are effective enough, and our faith fervent enough, there is no mountain too large for the Christian to move. The key biblical principle for securing God's blessings, for Gothard, is crying out in sincere faith. God desires to answer our prayers that he might bring more glory to himself. Gothard stresses the glory of God and his sovereignty over all things, and his desire to bless his children when they pray to him in the manner he desires. To quote Gothard, "Humble yourself and cry aloud to Him with all your heart. He will hear you, just as He has promised. And your life will begin to change from that hour."[20]

Bruce Wilkinson

Founder and President of Walk Thru the Bible Ministries, Dr. Bruce Wilkinson is recognized as a bible scholar throughout the Evangelical community. Dr. Howard Hendricks, a professor at Dallas Theological Seminary, writes "If you long to live your life the way it is meant to be lived in Christ, *The Prayer of Jabez* is a must read." Wilkinson has also written two follow- up books to *The Prayer of Jabez* called *Secrets of the Vine* and *A Life God Rewards*, which themselves have spawned an industry, including *Prayer of Jabez* bible studies, devotionals, calendars, journals, and special editions of the book for women, children, and teenagers.

Who is Wilkinson's God?

God, for Wilkinson, is the keeper of a storehouse of blessings that he is ready to dispense to all those who approach him in prayer - with the right words. God desires that we live a blessed life, full of everything needed to live that life to the fullest. At the very beginning of his book, Wilkinson says, "The little book you're holding is about what happens when ordinary Christians decide to reach for an extraordinary life - which, as it turns out, is exactly the kind God promises."[21] The blessed life, however, is not necessarily a life of material possessions and every pleasure the heart desires. Wilkinson is not suggesting that "you should ask God for a Cadillac, a six figure income, or some other material sign that you have found a way to cash in on your connection with Him."[22] Rather, Wilkinson believes God rewards a life committed to him and to his purposes with fulfillment and contentment.

Wilkinson's Understanding of Prayer

We pray because, in a word, "God favors those who ask."[23] If we wish to have all the blessings that God has in store for us, we must ask. Again, in Wilkinson's words, "If you don't ask for His blessing, you forfeit those that come to you only when you ask."[24] To pray is to go to God with our needs. But those needs should not be selfish, but rather reflect God's needs. The chief of those needs is of course the expansion of our own Christian ministry, for his glory. We should want nothing more and nothing less than what God wants for us. If what we want is to give glory to God, than there is nothing that we could ask for that God would not want to give to us. So long as we know the key to asking him properly.

Wilkinson writes, "If you were to ask me what sentence - other than my prayer for salvation has revolutionized my life and ministry the most, I would tell you that it was the cry of Jabez."[25] It is not enough that we pray, or that we cry out aloud, or even that we learn a model for prayer. There is a particular prayer that will always break through to God. In fact, Wilkinson actually writes, "I want to teach you how to pray a daring prayer that God always answers."[26] This is the prayer of Jabez, as recorded in the 1 Chronicles 4:10[a]. This prayer in itself cannot be a mantra, however. It does not work, in the

---

[a] Jabez called upon the God of Israel, saying, "Oh that you would bless me and enlarge my border, and that your hand might be with me, and that you would keep me from harm so that it might not bring me pain!" And God granted what he asked. (1 Ch 4:10)

language of the Lutheran dogmaticians, *ex opere operato*. God does not answer the prayer simply because we prayed its words. We must also commit to acting on it. "And, with a handful of core commitments on your part, you can proceed from this day forward with the confidence and expectation that your heavenly Father will bring it to pass for you."[27]

Jabez' prayer contains four petitions, each of which Wilkinson elaborates. First, we pray that God would bless us, and bless us indeed. It is okay to be selfish because we are being selfish in the cause of God. To be blessed and blessed indeed, writes Wilkinson, is to have "the unhindered forces of heaven... accomplishing God's perfect will - through you."[28] Second, we should pray that God would enlarge our territory, or expand our boundaries. We pray that God would make it possible for us to reach more people, touch more people, with God's power. God cannot ordinarily do this. "What he's waiting for is the invitation."[29] We also pray that God's hand would be with us in the endeavor's God has placed in front of us. "As God's chosen, blessed sons and daughters, we are expected to attempt something large enough that failure is guaranteed... unless God steps in."[30] Lastly, we should pray that God would keep us from evil. While temptation itself is not a sin, we should pray that God would keep us away from temptation, that we might be free from sin. Freedom from sin is essential for breaking through to the abundant life God has in store for us. In fact, "The only thing that can break this cycle of abundant living is sin, because sin breaks the flow of God's power."[31]

Praying for a Miracle

In the end, *The Prayer of Jabez* is not so much about God as it is about the individual. Prayer does not in any way serve God. Neither does it especially serve to strengthen the individual's relationship with God. Instead, it is a tool given by God for Christians to use to open God's spiritual storehouse. Certainly, the focus is on spiritual blessings that will give God glory, not temporal blessings. Wilkinson does clearly state this:

> Do we really understand how far the American Dream is from God's dream for us? We're steeped in a culture that worships freedom, independence, personal rights and the pursuit of pleasure. We respect people who sacrifice to get what they want. But to be a living sacrifice? To be crucified to self?[32]

But in the end, the goal of praying is to give God greater glory through the pray-er. The believer does not pray that God might be glorified through suffering, through his Word, or through someone else's work, but through the believer's ministry and efforts. The goal of prayer is to have God working miracles through the believer.

Hank Hannegraf

Hank Hanegraaff is the head of the Christian Research Institute (CRI), the host of "The Bible Answer Man" radio broadcast, and a self-appointed watchdog of Evangelical orthodoxy. His books on apologetics include *The Face that Demonstrates the Farce of Evolution* and *Resurrection*. His book, *The Prayer of Jesus*, followed closely on the heels of the publication of *The Prayer of Jabez* and seeks to respond to some of the claims made by Wilkinson in his book. Former Nixon administration official and head of Prison Ministries Charles Colson writes, "You'll find this book timely and richly rewarding."

Who is Hannegraf's God?

Following the suit of other Evangelical books, Hanegraaff has little to say about God and his persons. God is certainly viewed as the Sovereign Lord, omnipresent, omniscient and omnipotent. He is the "sovereign Creator." We are urged, as Christians, to give proper honor and adoration to the God of Creation. The language of Luther is also used, in that Hanegraaff writes, "God cares for (us) as a father cares for his own dear children."[33] 37 God also promises to hear the prayers of his children, and to answer them as he sees fit.

How Does Hannegraf Understand Prayer?

Prayer is not primarily supplication. Certainly prayer should never be supplication for selfish or self-aggrandizing reasons. Hanegraaff writes, "The goal of prayer should never be the roaring approval of the crowds."[34] The Christian does not pray in order to break through to a better or higher level of Christian life. A Christian prays because that is what a Christian does. "Prayer does not simply maintain the Christian life, it is the Christian life, reduced to its barest essence."[35] A Christian is one who is in union and communion with God through Jesus Christ. To be in communion with someone, we must have some form of communication. God longs for communication with us. That is the primary purpose of prayer. In our communication with God, we learn to trust him above all things. Hanegraaff stresses that it is through prayer that our faith and trust in God is strengthened. Prayer is not merely an expression of our faith, but a tool for maintaining faith. "Prayer becomes a means through which we learn to lean more heavily upon him and less heavily upon ourselves."[36]

Hanegraaff borrows from Lewis' writings on prayer to explain the paradox between God's omniscience and the value of petitionary prayer. Lewis sees God as providing the general script for existence, within which humans are allowed a limited amount of improvisation. Our Christian works and prayers are part of that improvisation, and God takes them into account. In Hanegraaff's words, "the work we do and the prayers we utter both produce results."[37] Like Gothard and Wilkinson, Hanegraaff does not dwell long on the question of free will and determinism, but simply assumes human free agency and God's omnipotence as accepted dogmas not worth delving into.

Hanegraaff does introduce the Scripture as an important factor in prayer. First of all, prayer should flow out of Scripture and God's will as expressed therein. Hanegraaff writes "the prayer of faith must always be rooted in Scripture."[38] He also encourages using the Psalms as a basis for prayer. Certainly, as the title of the book suggests, Hanegraaff recommends the Lord's Prayer itself. Not, in his words, as a "prayer mantra" but as a "prayer manner."[39] Second, he urges all Christians to study the Scriptures in order to be better able to know when the Holy Spirit is speaking. He advocated quiet times of listening: "I encourage you to develop the discipline of listening for the voice of God."[40] In order to be able to discern what is of God and what is not, he urges praying Christians to know their Bible well. "The more you meditate on Scripture, the clearer the voice of the Master will be within the sounds of silence."[41] Third, he recommends using a prayer pattern similar to Luther's, allowing for adoration, confession, thanksgiving and then supplication. Confession of sins is important, because unconfessed sins can interfere with the effectiveness of prayer.

Prayer as Proper Technique

Hanegraaff attempts to provide an antidote to Wilkinson's *The Prayer of Jabez* by stressing prayer as relationship, not merely supplication. He does this by using the Lord's Prayer as a model for all prayers, much as Wilkinson takes apart Jabez' prayer but with a slightly different aim in mind. However, Hanegraaff falls into many of the same traps, including the trap of the prayer "technique:" "Turn the page," he writes at the beginning of his book, "and discover the very first secret of praying Jesus' way."[42] Hanegraaff does use language similar to the Small Catechism, such as his references to our dear Father who loves us as dear children, and the battle against devil, world and flesh. But he also insists that unconfessed sin remains an obstacle to prayer, addresses God as "Sovereign Creator" more than as Redeemer, and focuses more on the benefits of prayer as a relationship with God than as an expression of trust in him.

Stormie Omartian

Stormie Omartian is a former actress and singer come Christian author and speaker. She has written ten best-selling books on prayer, including *The Power of a Praying Wife, The Power of a Praying Husband* and *The Power of a Praying Parent*. She has also written an autobiography detailing the abuse she suffered as a child from her mother called *Stormie*. She has co-written a musical called *Child of the Promise* with her husband, Grammy-award winning artist Michael Omartian. She currently resides with him and their children in Nashville.

Who is Omartian's God?

Omartian structures the first part of her book around the three-fold nature of God. She wants her readers to see God as a Trinity; however, her understanding of the Trinity tends toward modalism. For Omartian, God has three "aspects" or "parts," much like an apple has a peel, a core and flesh. In fact Omartian uses this very analogy for God, which she claims to have drawn from a Concordia Publishing House children's book.[43] Omartian speaks of God "as Savior, as Father, and as Holy Spirit." Nowhere is Jesus directly identified with God. He is the Son of God, salvation was accomplished through him, and receiving him into yourself is the only way of being saved by God, but he is only one part or aspect of God. Omartian writes that God "is Emmanuel, the God who is with you right now to the degree you acknowledge Him in your life."[44]

God knows all things that we need, has our best interests at heart, and desires only the best for us. Omartian describes the Bible as "God's love letters to you... They say, 'This is how much I love you.'"[45] God wants us, out of our free will, to reciprocate his love, so that he

Not As We Ought 67
Charles St-Onge

can bless us in our lives. She quotes one of her pastors as saying, "God knows our thoughts, but He responds to our prayers. We have to come to a place of realizing that prayer is a privilege that is always ours, but the power in prayer is always His. *Without God, we can't do it. Without us, God won't do it.*"[46]

What is Omartian's Understanding of Prayer?

Prayer, as illustrated by the quote from her pastor, is necessary if God is going to work on our behalf. As we learn to pray, God is able to do more and more on our behalf, and work more of his power in our life. Prayer is absolutely essential for our growth as Christians. Omartian writes, "Without prayer, the full purpose God has for you can't happen."[47] She also writes, "I can possess only as much of what He has for me as I am willing to secure with my obedience."[48] Christians obey God chiefly by praying.

The blessings that God desires for us center chiefly around 1) being in line with God's will for our life and 2) receiving the inner joy that comes from being in God's will. God's will for our life is not to be confused with the obedience to his requirements that God expects. Rather, God's will is more like a day by day diary in which we find written every aspect of our life laid out in advance by God to maximize our happiness. This happiness comes, first of all, from receiving Christ and being born again. Then we have "that inner, happy confidence that there is nothing that can successfully resist the inevitability of Christ's certain triumph in me."[49] But if we do not continue to build on that initial relationship, we will fall out of God's will and lose that inner peace. "After I came to know the Lord and experienced that warm, close, rich feeling of walking with God, I still feel back into some old, familiar bad habits."[50] The Christian must always be on guard against sin, which is usually the prime culprit for "cutting off the possibilities God has for your life."[51]

True prayer consists in knowing how to come to God and address him. Once we discover these new ways of approaching God, we increase our likelihood of receiving everything God has to give us, and remaining in God's will for our life. That will is "there for each one of us, but we have to take the necessary steps to find it." We each "have the power within us to reach our full potential."[52] Some of the prayer steps we need to take include knowing and opening our life to the various aspects of God: Father, Savior, and Holy Spirit. The Christian should, for example, "determine that you will not close yourself off from the Father who loves you."[53] The Christian should also "acknowledge the Holy Spirit's existence and then be open to His working."[54] Understanding the various names, titles, and roles of God presented in the Scripture will also open us up to receive more of his blessings. For example, if we need hope, we should address God as the One who is our Hope. Likewise with comfort, strength, and other needs. Omartian provides lists of names to use for calling on God. "When we acknowledge Him by those names, we invite Him to be those things to us."[55] Faith itself is a gift that can be increased by proper prayer. "Faith is first a decision, then an exercise in obedience, then a gift from God as it is multiplied."[56] As we learn to approach God through his aspects and his characteristics, we reap the reward of a richer, more fulfilling life.

Obedience to the Lord is another aspect of a prayerful life. Omartian urges us to receive all of God's abundance and power, for example, by tithing 10%, being baptized at the earliest opportunity, and communing. Communion and baptism are important, not for what they communicate or do for us, but because they show God our obedience and help us remain in his will:

> Just as there is no magic in the water of baptism, there is also nothing magical in the wine, grape juice, bread of cracker of Communion. The power lies in our participation... If you

can't get to a Communion service in your church, then do it at home by yourself.[57]

Prayer as Personal Empowerment

Omartian's take on prayer could be called the "video game" approach. Just as in a video game players earn points to progress to the next level, so too in prayer do Christians receive increased blessings as they learn to progress through levels of understandings of prayer. One learns to unlock the secrets of the different aspects of God, then the different parts of one's life that can be handed over to God, each time increasing the blessings earned. The chief blessing in Omartian's case is to remain in God's will. If we sin, we fall out of God's will, and lose the "warm, close, rich feeling" of walking with the Lord.[58]

Bill Hybels

Bill Hybels is the head pastor of Willow Creek Church outside Chicago, Illinois, currently one of the most attended churches in the United States. The church offers several workshops throughout the year for those wishing to emulate Willow Creek's success in reaching "the unchurched." Bill has written or co-authored numerous books, including *Courageous Leadership, Christians in the Marketplace, Seven Wonders of the Spiritual World* and *Becoming a Contagious Christian. Too Busy Not To Pray* is his first book specifically devoted to prayer.

Who is Hybels' God?

Unlike Omartian, and like Hanegraaff, Gothard and Wilkinson, Hybels does not spend much time talking about the nature of God in relation to prayer. What he does emphasize about God is his omnipotence and his sovereignty. In fact, Hybels believes true prayer is impossible without first recognizing God's omnipotence. "Whatever it takes for you to own the doctrine of God's omnipotence, do it. Until you own it, you will be a faint-hearted prayer."[59] This belief plays out in the forms of address found for God in Hybels own prayers. For example,

Hybels says that he begins some of his prayers by reminding himself that "I'm praying to the Creator of the world, the King of the universe, the all-powerful, all-knowing, all-faithful God."[60]

This view of God tends to sideline Christ. Although Jesus is important for salvation, he is viewed mostly as a stepping stone for reaching God, the one who has the true power. Hybels even offers an apology for the need to pray in Jesus' name, reminding his readers "Although you pray in Jesus' name, you can be sure that your requests go directly to God."[61] In fact, God's work in Jesus would only be complete when God sent the Holy Spirit into the world. Before that, "God's presence in Christ... still lacked something."[62] Once the Holy Spirit was sent, God's presence - salvation - became "real. You can feel it. It's with you wherever you go."[63] It is this presence of God in the Christian's life that prayer is intended to expand and enhance.

What is Hybels' Understanding of Prayer?

Prayer is the means by which the Christian opens herself to the blessings of God. These blessings can come in various ways. For example, Hybels writes that in response to prayer "God would bless me with special portion of his Spirit, a material item I had been wanting or a warm new a relationship."[64]

But in order for these blessings to properly accrue to the Christian, he or she must be ready to pray. The relationship between God's power and the recipient of that power must be cooperative. In fact, that is the very word Hybels uses, as he writes in God's voice, "Just a reasonable amount of cooperation, and I will pour out my blessings on you."[65]

The chief blessing, of course, is an awareness of God's presence. This awareness is a feeling that in and of itself brings many benefits, according to Hybels. The greatest benefit is "to feel God's peace in our hearts."[66] The second blessing is being aware of what Hybels calls "God's leadings." Hybels spends the better part of his book talking about these leadings, whereby God directs his followers, audibly or inaudibly, toward the path that his will desires them to take. Receiving and responding in obedience to these leadings. Hybels writes, "Your growth as a Christian depends on receiving and responding to leadings."[67] The Christian opens himself or herself to these leadings through a prayer life that includes both speaking to God and listening for God's answer.

According to Hybels, prayer should be secret, sincere, and specific. Prayer should be secret, in that it is something between God and the believer alone, and not to be done for public glory or admiration. It should also be sincere, by which Hybels means it should come from the heart. Hybels warns of falling into "meaningless repetition" of "clichés." The Lord's Prayer, Hybels warns, can become such a cliché. "The Lord's Prayer is an excellent model, but it was never intended to be a magical incantation to get God's attention. Jesus didn't give his prayer as a paragraph to be recited."[68] Prayer should also be specific. Hybels uses the Lord's Prayer as an example of specificity, briefly outlining all of the things which should be included in prayer, including adoration of God as sovereign, majestic and omnipotent.

Hybels also recommends the ACTS acronym as a model for prayer: Adoration, Confession, Thanksgiving and Supplication. Hybels writes that the best way to adore God is to list his attributes. When in need of mercy, praise God for his mercy. When in need of help, praise God for his guidance. Confession is also a key component of prayer, for sins are one thing that will block your prayers from reaching God. "If you let even a little sin into your heart, it's going to contaminate your prayers."[69] The point of confessing sins is to eventually not have any to confess:

About the fifth day in a row that you have to call yourself a
liar, a greedy person, a manipulator, or whatever, you say to
yourself, 'I'm tired of admitting that. With God's power, I've
got to root it out of my life.'[70]

Other than sins of commission or omission, doubt will also block
prayer from reaching God and render him unwilling to provide you
with leadings. "If your prayers have clouds of doubt hanging over
them, they won't get anywhere."[71]

Prayer as Key to Life's Blessings

Like the other Evangelical authors presented here, Hybels is chiefly
concerned with the blessings that prayer can unlock for the
Christian. God is a sovereign, majestic, and omnipotent being who is
prepared to help with all your needs - if only you ask properly.
Without an adequate prayer life, the Christian cannot benefit from all
that God has in store for them. Like the early church, Hybels
emphasizes the need to be leading a moral and generally sinless life
in order for prayers to be answered.

Conclusion

There are several themes which run through all of these books and
place them clearly in the same theological tradition. The first of these
is the emphasis on God as Sovereign Creator, not as Redeemer. The
goal of prayer is participation in the creative work of God in our own
life, rather than maintaining a reconciling relationship with a Savior.
Prayer is a means through which the Christian participates alongside
God in accomplishing his goals for the world, but more specifically
his goals for the Christian's own life. The theme of sinner/Redeemer
does not figure prominently in any of the literature, except when the
author speaks of his or her own conversion experience. Once the
believer has been redeemed, she moves on to a more meaningful

relationship with God where his power is revealed in her life whenever she asks - properly, of course - in prayer.

A corollary to this theme is the view of sin as an obstacle to true prayer. Rather than sin being a motivation for prayer to the One who can remove that sin and strengthen against the devil, the world, and the flesh, sin is seen as something to be dealt with prior to effective prayer. Confession of sin and a promise of amendment is not part and parcel of prayer, but a prelude to truly effective prayer. Every Christian, then, must be constantly on the lookout for unconfessed sin in their lives, lest their prayers be less effective than might otherwise be the case. This view does not seem to be all that different from that of the early church, where the answers the Christian received to prayer were dependant on the moral quality of his life.

The other theme that flows through all the books, although it is not as prominent in Hanegraaff's, is the view that prayer is the key to having great things happen in the Christian's life. All the authors are especially concerned about how prayer can mobilize the Christian for "ministry." It is certainly true that God is great, and can accomplish great things. The life of the Christian should be one of trust that God will work powerfully through his Church to accomplish, what in the end, is his mission: to seek the lost, to heal the sick, to bind up the broken hearted. Cardinal Suhard wrote, "To be a witness means to live in such a way that one's life would make no sense if God did not exist."[72]

Yet the approach to witnessing described in these books is, to coin a phrase, cross-less. True prayer is to transform the Christian's life into one of quality, meaning, and abundance - not necessarily material abundance, but certainly one of emotional joy. How then does one make sense of Christ's demand that the Christian pick up his cross and follow him? (Matthew 10:38)[b]. The life of Christian witness is not always one of obvious meaning, abundance, and fulfillment. Often it is one of suffering, at least in the eyes of the world. To describe any prayer technique as a means for "breaking through to the blessed life" is not to tell the whole story.

Which leads to the last theme, the idea that prayer is the means through which God's blessings are released. This theme is found in all the books, in different forms, and with different emphases, but present nonetheless. While blatant requests for "material abundance" for the sake of abundance are rejected by all the authors, especially Hybels and Wilkinson, it is a qualified rejection. If the abundance is required to expand the Kingdom of God, one is certainly permitted - even commanded - to ask. If the blessings the believer is to seek in prayer are not material, then one must ask what exactly these blessings are. Forgiveness is certainly not part of prayer, as was mentioned earlier. Eternal life is not spoken of with great fervor by any of the authors: their worldview seems to be focused primarily on this world. If God's blessings are not material wants, forgiveness or eternal life, what remains but emotional and spiritual fulfillment?

This is exactly what the authors mean by "blessing." Prayer, when done correctly, makes you feel good! It gives shape and form to your spiritual life, assures you that you are following God's plan for your future, and grants you a sense of purpose and fulfillment in your life. Here the Evangelicals follow a path not all that dissimilar to Schleiermacher, being concerned more with how God is perceived and felt within than God's actual moral demands. The roots of their views on prayer can also be traced indirectly to Calvin. The goal of the Christian life is looking ahead to future victory rather than back

---

[b] And whoever does not take his cross and follow me is not worthy of me. (Mt 10:38)

to God's past victory on the cross. Prayer is not focused on expressing trust in God to save us, as he saved his people in the past, but rather on bringing us fulfillment and purpose now and into the future - although that future does not seem to explicitly include a life in the next world. There is perhaps no more fitting critique of this view of prayer than the one offered by a musical group within the Evangelical tradition:

> "I think of the things I do / I need nothing more from you / Just to be forgiven / Is enough for me."
> - *Life in the First Degree, Adam Again*

---

[1] Stormie Omartian. *Praying God's Will for Your Life*. (Nashville: Nelson Publishers, 2001).

[2] Bruce Wilkinson. *The Prayer of Jabez*. (Sisters, OR: Multnomah, 2000).

[3] Bill Hybels. *Too Busy Not To Pray*. (Downers Grove, IL: InterVarsity Press, 1988).

[4] Hank Hanegraaff. *The Prayer of Jesus*. (Nashville: W Publishing Group, 2001).

[5] Bill Gothard. *The Power of Crying Out*. (Sisters, OR: Multnomah Publishers, 2002).

[6] Gothard, 86.

[7] Gothard, 23.

[8] Gothard, 37.

[9] Gothard, 49.

[10] Gothard, 25.

[11] Gothard, 19.

[12] Gothard, 12.

[13] Gothard, 90.

[14] Gothard, 66.

[15] Gothard, 75.

[16] Gothard, 77.

[17] Gothard, 12.

[18] Gothard, 42.

[19] Gothard, 42.

[20] Gothard, 91.

[21] Bruce Wilkinson. *The Prayer of Jabez*. (Sisters, OR: Multnomah, 2000), 7.

[22] Wilkinson, 24.

[23] Wilkinson, 76.

[24] Wilkinson, 27.

[25] Wilkinson, 11.

[26] Wilkinson, 7.

[27] Wilkinson, 17.

[28] Wilkinson, 25.

[29] Wilkinson, 41.

[30] Wilkinson, 47.

[31] Wilkinson, 85.

[32] Wilkinson, 70.

[33] Hank Hanegraaff. *The Prayer of Jesus.* (Nashville: W Publishing Group, 2001), 57.
[34] Hanegraaff, 57.
[35] Hanegraaff, 10.
[36] Hanegraaff, 26.
[37] Hanegraaff, 29.
[38] Hanegraaff, 23.
[39] Hanegraaff, 35.
[40] Hanegraaff, 85.
[41] Hanegraaff, 87.
[42] Hanegraaff, 3.
[43] Joanne Marxhausen. *Three in One.* (Saint Louis: Concordia Publishing House, 1973).
[44] Stormie Omartian. *Praying God's Will for Your Life.* (Nashville: Nelson Publishers, 2001), 52.
[45] Omartian, 69.
[46] Omartian, 75 (italics hers).
[47] Omartian, 81.
[48] Omartian, 124.
[49] Omartian, 90.
[50] Omartian, 99.
[51] Omartian, 134.
[52] Omartian, 22.
[53] Omartian, 31.
[54] Omartian, 35.
[55] Omartian, 51.
[56] Omartian, 169.
[57] Omartian, 163.
[58] Omartian, 99.
[59] Bill Hybels. *Too Busy Not To Pray.* (Downers Grove, IL: InterVarsity Press, 1988), 35.
[60] Hybels, 67.
[61] Hybels, 36.
[62] Hybels, 146.
[63] Hybels, 147.
[64] Hybels, 24.
[65] Hybels, 70.
[66] Hybels, 151.
[67] Hybels, 114.
[68] Hybels, 47.
[69] Hybels, 90.
[70] Hybels, 56.
[71] Hybels, 94.
[72] *A New Handbook of Christian Theology.* Donald W. Musser and Joseph L. Price, eds. (Nashville: Abingdon Press, 1992), 162.

Chapter 5: Prayer and Modern Lutherans

The quantity of writings of the contemporary Lutheran community on prayer does not come close to matching the Evangelical community. However there have been a number of books on prayer written in recent times by those who consider themselves in the Lutheran confessional tradition. These books are worth considering on their own, to compare them with Luther's own thought as well as to the writings of their contemporaries in other traditions

Among these writers four stand out, spanning the better part of the twentieth century. The first is Ole Hallesby, represents the independent Norwegian Lutheran movement, a pietistic movement within the Norwegian state church. This movement stressed spiritual experiences and Christian commitment as being of equivalent in importance to doctrinal correctness. Walter Wangerin, Jr., a prolific writer, represents the more liberal position within Lutheranism, from an American perspective. The theological emphases of this community are very similar to those of the Scandinavian pietistic community. Jane Fryar represents the conservative Lutheranism typified by the Lutheran Church - Missouri Synod. While the core Lutheran doctrine of justification by grace through faith is upheld in this community, it is occasionally at the expense of the objective character of God's dealing with his people in the preached Word and the sacraments. A brief examination of Dietrich Bonhoeffer's thoughts on prayer is also undertaken. Bonhoeffer represents the confessing Lutheran community of Germany during the Second World War, with its own pietistic emphases. Lastly, Francis Pieper's discussion of prayer in his *Christian Dogmatics* is presented, representing the orthodox dogmatic tradition of Lutheranism.

Ole Hallesby

Dr. Ole Hallesby was a professor of the Independent Theological Seminary in Oslo, Norway. He was a leader in the resistance to the German occupation of Norway in the Second World War, and spent time in a concentration camp for his efforts. Hallesby, in response to the liberalization ofthe Norwegian church, "advocated a theology that combined orthodoxy and pietism."[1] Hallesby felt he was preparing Norway for a period of revival expected in the early 20 century. His other works include a dogmatics, a work entitled *Why I Am a Christian*, and *Prayer*. This last is considered a classic by many in and outside the Lutheran community, despite its age.

Who is Hallesby's God?

Hallesby believes that God is present to the believer chiefly in his son, Jesus Christ, through the working of the Holy Spirit. God is, above all else, our Creator and Redeemer who wishes to give us all that we need. Indeed, Hallesby writes, "He has all that we need, and there is nothing that He would rather do than impart to us His gifts."[2] This love of God toward us is seen most clearly, not in creation, but in the work and person of Jesus Christ. "When Jesus hears our prayers and intervenes in our distress, He does so because His love toward us is free and unmerited, and because He by His suffering and death has purchased and won for us all that we need."[3] There is nothing we can do to earn God's love and care; he showers that love and care on believer and unbeliever alike.

However, the believer can receive God's love in a personal way, because he opens the door for God to work through him. Hallesby believes that "Jesus reveals clearly that aspect of God's perfect love according to which He gives everybody all that He can persuade them, in one way or another, to accept."[4] God will not force anyone to accept his love and care; rather, he stands at the door and knocks, and desires that we give him admittance, to do for us all that he would like to do. Christ "enters in of his own accord, because He desires to come in. And He enters in wherever He is not denied admittance."[5] Even so, God's love is such that unbelievers can also call upon and receive his love and care in a special way. Hallesby writes, "God, at times, grants the prayers of the unconverted for the same reason that He showers other blessings upon them, namely, because he loves them and desires to save them."[6]

In fact, man's desire to admit God or deny him admittance is a determining factor in world affairs. Although God is certainly omnipotent, he has chosen to work through the decisions and prayers of fallible human creatures. Therefore the prayers and work of the Christian certainly do matter, and have temporal consequences. "The attitude which man takes is the vital factor in determining whether the world shall attain its goal or not. God has voluntarily bound Himself to man in His government of the world..."[7]

What is Hallesby's Understanding of Prayer

Prayer, then, is of great importance. The Christian should never feel that his prayers are of little value, on account of God's omniscience, because God will bring certain things to pass only under the influence of prayer. In Hallesby's own words, "God has made Himself voluntarily dependent also upon our prayer."[8] Prayer has an impact not only on our own interior spiritual life, but alsoon the actions of God in the world. But neither should the impact of prayer on the personal life of the Christian be ignored. "Prayer is the breath of the soul, the organ by which we receive Christ into our parched and withered hearts."[9] Without prayer, the Christian and her faith shrivel and die. Prayer is a necessary part of the Christian life. This is because Christ requires admittance into our hearts to be able to exercise his power. "Prayer has one function, and that is to answer 'Yes' when He knocks, to open the soul and give Him the opportunity to bring us the answer."[10] Though at times the answer on our part may be weak, full of doubt, and marred by our own sin, it is enough. Christ comes in, and works all in all in us and through us. Without our giving admittance, however, God in Christ is not able to work.

What is it, chiefly, that God works in us? Certainly, salvation, but also the comfort and joy that go along with being saved by Christ and his work. "Prayer should be the means by which I, at all times, receive all that I need, and, for this reason, be my daily refuge, my daily consolation, my daily joy, my source of rich and inexhaustible joy in life."[11] Prayer brings with it "the sense of the Lord's nearness, which then fills our souls, is greater than any other peace, joy, inner satisfaction, or security which we have known."[12] This peace, in turn, helps us deal with the adversity we are sure to face in the world. Sorrow, anxiety and all other concerns lose their sting when the Christian communicates with the Lord in prayer. The goal of prayer, in so far as it opens the door to God's work, is to prepare us to do his will in the world. God's will is that we diminish, that we might love our neighbor as ourselves and be Christ's servants in the world:

> Every day Christianity cannot be practiced unless we incessantly receive into our lives that supply of spiritual power which is necessary in order to preserve within us that spirit which is willing to deny self, to serve others, to endure wrong, and to let others have the last word.[13]

Prayer is also the means of confessing our sins to God, so that he might eradicate them from us. Certainly Hallesby does not see sin as an obstacle to prayer. But sin is something that the Lord must deal with, and does deal with in prayer. In quiet times of prayer, while the Christian is listening to God, God reveals sins, brings them to light, and deals with them by means of his Gospel. "It is the work of the Spirit to convict of sin. The quiet hour of prayer is one of the most favorable opportunities He has in which to speak to us seriously."[14]

In fact, when the Spirit reveals our sin to the Christian, the Christian's motivation to pray should increase. Not because of a need to show increased obedience, but out of thankfulness for God's mercy and forgiveness.

> When the Spirit shows us the hardness, the slothfulness, and the indifference of our hearts toward prayer, we now become anxious and confused no longer. Instead they become added incentives to prayer, that is, the opening of our heart's door to give Jesus access to all our distress and our impotence.[15]

One cannot pray without also recognizing one's helplessness. Prayer is the crying out of the soul that knows it cannot survive without God. "Prayer and helplessness are inseparable. Only he who is helpless can truly pray."[16] Whether faith is absolutely necessary for such a cry of helplessness to be effective before the throne of God is unclear in Hallesby's writing. On the one hand, he writes, "Without faith our helplessness will be only a vain cry of distress in the night." But faith need not be perfect, or even of a certain quality, to ensure our prayers are heard. The smallest prayer demonstrates that at least a weak faith is present, and Christ is able to do the rest. "...It is blessed to know that we have faith enough when we bring our needs to Jesus and leave them with Him."[17] Hallesby stresses that unbelief and doubt are quite different things, and one can pray even though harboring doubts. Elsewhere, Hallesby speaks of occasions when even the prayers of the "unconverted" are heard by God.

Before God the Christian should pray for herself and for her neighbors, asking God to work his will through her and in her neighbors. She is not to worry whether what she is praying for is too great for God or too unimportant. "We are to pray. God Himself will take care of the hearing and the fulfillment."[18] In prayer the Christian is also to listen to God, not just speak to him. Prayer is conversation.

"Everyone who is experienced in prayer knows that to listen quietly and humbly for what the Spirit of prayer says, requires continued and powerful wrestling."[19]

Prayer as the Vehicle for the Orthodox God's Work

Hallesby, desiring to blend orthodox Lutheran dogma with pietistic spiritual sentiment, has done exactly that on the subject of prayer. God remains the triune God of orthodox dogma, and even more importantly is the God who rescues and saves his people: a God who is God for them. Jesus is fully God, and is much the subject and object of prayer as the heavenly Father and the Holy Spirit. The Christian is urged to pray for God's power, not in order to have a more fulfilling and blessed life, but in order to become more like Christ. Yet prayer remains a means for God's work. Without prayer, God can neither gain admittance into our lives to improve our spiritual condition, nor can God work through us to accomplish his will. The pietistic need to preserve free will in spiritual matters subordinates God's work of salvation to the actions and prayers of human beings. Furthermore, the idea of prayer being a means to a more "fulfilling" Christian life is added to prayer as the response of faith.

Walter Wangerin

Walter Wangerin, Jr, is currently the writer-in-residence at Valparaiso University. Born and raised in a Lutheran parsonage, Wangerin also served for many years as pastor of Grace Lutheran Church in Evansville, Indiana. He is the author of numerous award-winning and best-selling books, including *The Book of the Dun Cow*, *Ragman and Other Cries of Faith*, *Miz Lil and the Chronicles of Grace* and *As For Me and My House*. His book *Whole Prayer* is part of a series of books on the Christian life sponsored by Zondervan Publishing and Eugene Peterson, himself the author of several books on prayer.

Who is Wangerin's God?

For Wangerin, God is above all the caring Father who comforts and forgives his children. He uses familial language for God several times throughout the book and nowhere more poignantly than when he is writing about someone approaching death, from God's perspective: "O my child, I love you. Rest in my refuge. Rest in my strength. Rest, and afterward - sleep."[20] There is nowhere where God is not, and no time when he is absent. It is this very omnipresence of God that frees the Christian to act boldly in the world, following in the footsteps of Christ. Wangerin writes:

> Even so is the invisible Spirit with us still, everywhere and every-when. Even so is his very presence the consolation that answers prayer; for his presence allows us to decide anything according to our best intelligence; for there is no where we can go away from his Spirit.[21]

It is God's love and his promise to always hear us that gives prayer its power. God's answer to the Christian's prayer is not dependent on anything within him, but only on the character of God. God himself empowers his prayer. In fact, it is "God's love (that) is the power that receives our voice."[22] Wangerin writes "the power of prayer is not in us, that we speak. It is in God, that he listens!"[23]

In several places Wangerin identifies God's power with Jesus, his work and his person, and with God's forgiveness. God's power is not seen solely in his work in creation, in thunder and lightning, in earthquakes, in personal miracles. Certainly God's power is also visible there, but for Wangerin God's power is in forgiveness. "The God who forgives will also deliver you from your troubles," not the sovereign God who created all things and works all things mightily.[24]

Wangerin's Understanding of Prayer

The purpose of prayer is not supplication, or opening a door, but building a relationship between God and ourselves. This relationship is one of trust and one of love. We trust God to provide for all our needs and not to abandon us. We love him because he has loved us in Christ. "Love and trust are the supreme purposes of prayer that we pray in loving trust to our dear Father, and that he answers out of his infinite store of merciful love."[25]

Wangerin again uses the relationship between a child and its parent as a pattern of the Christian's relationship with God. Wangerin writes:

> So let us say, little child, that your trust is waning... You say, 'The Lord has forsaken me.'... But straightaway, the light goes on in the hallway! Whether you see it or not, whether you hear it or not, God listens. God comes and attends you. God does this thing![26]

Prayer is a way of life for the Christian. It is the pulse and breath of the Christian, for it is in prayer that a relationship is established between the Christian and God. Wangerin advocates a regular discipline of prayer which serves to shape the believer's spirit, and becomes for her a way of life. Whole prayer, prayer that involves listening to God, living out his will, and speaking to him on a disciplined basis, "grows into the wholeness of divine relationship."[27]

Wangerin posits that prayer should follow a fourfold pattern. We speak, then God listens to our speaking. God then speaks, and we in turn listen to him. In speaking, the Christian demonstrates both love and trust in God. Children, when they come to their parents, "ask trusting. They manifest trust by asking. And trust presumes that God shall hear and, hearing, answer."[28] To guide this speaking, Wangerin recommends following the five-fold form of the traditional collect.

He also recommends using the Psalms, and the prayers of the Church as they have been collected throughout the age. But speaking prayers is only the first stage of the cycle of whole prayer. He reminds his readers of this by point out that "'Amen' does not conclude communication! It was never intended to."[29] Our prayer life continues with God's hearing our requests, and continues with God's speaking in turn to us.

For Wangerin, God speaks primarily, but not exclusively, through the Scripture. Wangerin describes the Bible as a repository of God's actions, from which we can see the pattern for how God might speak to us. Wangerin writes, "The Bible is God's dictionary! It presents both his words, his chosen language... and the meaning of those words."[30] God may, of course, speak directly through the Scripture itself, and we should be open to this speaking. "Listen for the Lord's voice as he begins to speak the old words newly..."[31] One of the best places to listen for God is in the Psalms.

By becoming familiar with Scripture, the Christian can properly interpret what God might be saying to her through his creation and through her fellow human beings. Otherwise, she may falsely believe to be hearing God's voice. Wangerin believes that if what the Christian believes to be divine communication is similar to a message in Scripture, and is not contradicted by Scripture, then the Christian can safely assume it to be a message from God. Such a message may come from any number of sources. Wangerin writes, for example, "Creation vibrates both with praise for God and with the song of God in answer."[32]

Prayer as Listening to the God who Loves

Wangerin emphasizes the love of God for his creatures as comparable to the love of parents for their child. Prayer, then, is the communication that establishes the relationship between the heavenly Father and his children. The Christian speaks to God in trust, expecting an answer. The Christian should not be paralyzed in indecision, however, in fear of not following God's will. Rather, the Christian should ask for strength, in whatever situation he finds himself, to act as Christ would act. Prayer also includes listening for God's voice, and evaluating that voice against the Scriptural records of God's character and his past revelations. The cycle of whole prayer, speaking and listening, continues without end throughout a Christian's life.

Jane Fryar

Jane Fryar was trained as a teacher at Concordia College, Seward, Nebraska, and recently received both a doctorate in organizational leadership from Regent University in Virginia, as well as an honorary doctorate from Concordia in Seward. She has authored several books on Christianity and teaching. She is the author of the *Today's Light* devotional booklets, *Feed My Sheep*, and conducts workshops on prayer throughout the Lutheran Church - Missouri Synod. Her book on prayer, *Armed and Dangerous*, is her first comprehensive book on the subject.

Who is Fryar's God?

God, for Fryar, is "no shriveled up Scrooge who peers down from heaven looking for ways to withhold His blessings and His help from us. Our God opens His heart and His hand to His children minute by minute, day by day, generation to generation."[33] God wants to give good gifts to his children, especially the gift of salvation, and the power to do good in the world. Fryar uses many superlatives to describe God, including but not limited to 'awesome,' 'kind' and 'wonderful.' God is "a powerful God, a loving God, and He delights in bringing hope, salvation and deliverance to people."[34]

But God and his will are most clearly visible in the person and work of Jesus Christ. It is Christ who makes prayer - indeed, any access to God at all - possible. Christ is the "One who has invited us to pray," and he can do so because he is the mediator between God and man. Christ is not incidental to God, but the revealer of everything that we know about him. "When God gave Jesus to die for you, He proved Himself trustworthy. The will of God to which Jesus assented... centered on our eternal good, our eternal life."[35] Furthermore, when we pray, we are not to focus on God and his majesty, but on Jesus and his glory. In Fryar's words, "Focus on Jesus. He is the Savior. He is the Healer. He is the Prince of Peace. He is the Wonderful Counselor. He is the giver of all good things."[36]

Fryar's Understanding of Prayer

In prayer, the Christian partners with God to accomplish his purposes on earth. Fryar makes it clear that God could accomplish his will without the participation of his creatures. However, in his grace he has made it possible for us to work alongside him in carrying out his work. He has chosen to "give us the privilege of partnership with Him in that work as we pray."[37] Through our intercessions, which are prompted and led by the Holy Spirit, we share in God's will and his work. Our prayers are important, then, because they impact what will occur in the lives of neighbors, strangers, and enemies. Fryar speaks out against those who believe prayer primarily shapes the pray-er, and does not change God's will or actions:

> Such people see prayer as a way God changes us and our attitudes, rather than as a way we can participate in His purposes for people or as a way we can influence events and

circumstances. How sad. How much peace and joy such people miss on their journey through life.[38]

God answers all prayers, even those of sinners such as us. God's answer to prayer is either "yes" or "I have something better in mind."[39] The Christian should take comfort in this fact, and be encouraged to pray, even if her prayer does not seem to be receiving an answer. In time, it will one way or the other.

The petitions of the Christian's prayer should be directed toward the work of God in the world, both through the pray-er and through others. The chief work of God, of course, is the spread of the Gospel. Fryar urges frequent prayers for all pastors, teachers and missionaries of the Church. It is these prayers that will be hardest, because it is these prayers that are most opposed by the Devil. These prayers will have an impact on us even if they do not directly include us by name.

> We intercede for our own service and for the service others give in Christ's name. As we do that, we obey God, we please God, we become more like Christ, we receive power for our service, and we participate in the coming of the Kingdom of Christ.[40]

The content of our prayers should be based on the Scriptures. Fryar recommends reflection on many different portions of the New and Old Testament as food for prayer. She also recommends the ACTS formula of Adoration, Confession, Thanksgiving and Supplication as a good directional aid for our prayer. As part of prayer, Christians listen for God's response to prayer through the Scriptures. "God speaks to us through His Word. We respond in praise, in worship, in confession, in petition."[41] If the Scriptures are the means through which God communicates with the Christian, prayer is then the means through which the Christian communicates with God. Fryar likens this cycle to breathing, the taking in of air and the breathing of air out. "The Scriptures shape us, and we in turn pray prayers forged by the Scriptures."[42]

Prayer Through God in Christ Jesus

For Fryar, God's character is defined by Christ. Jesus is the necessary focus of all our prayers. It is he who opened up access to the throne of grace by his death, and it is through him that prayers to God should be addressed. God has granted the possibility of our prayers affecting the lives of others as well as ourselves. This does not at all impinge on God's omnipotence, but reflects his grace and mercy toward us in Christ. The content of the Christian's prayers should be shaped by the Scriptures, through which God in turn speaks to the Christian. Prayer should be focused on strength for service, freedom from sin, and the expansion of the Kingdom of God on earth.

Dietrich Bonhoeffer

Dietrich Bonhoeffer was a German pastor who was executed by the Nazis in 1945, days before the end of the Second World War. He taught in the United States and pastored a church in London, eventually returning to Germany during the Nazi regime to lead the seminary of the Confessing Church. Many of his writings dealt with the need for Christian discipleship and what that entailed. These writings include *The Cost of Discipleship*, *Life Together* and *Act and Being*. Although Bonhoeffer did not write any specific work exclusively about prayer, works such as *The Cost of Discipleship* demonstrate that he held prayer in high esteem.

Who is Bonhoeffer's God?

God, for Bonhoeffer, is most clearly present and known in Christ. There is no avoiding the saturation of Bonhoeffer's works with language about Jesus. In his work *The Cost of Discipleship*, Bonhoeffer defines God as the one who calls us to discipleship in Jesus Christ.

Christ is the Word of God, and therefore also the revelation of the human situation vis-à-vis the Father and the Holy Spirit. God's desire is to see his creatures take up Christ's cross and follow him, and thereby to be restored to communion with him by his grace. However, only Christ's call to discipleship can bestow the grace that obedience requires. Bonhoeffer writes, "When Christ calls a man, he bids him come and die."[43] The Christian cannot kill himself, however. Discipleship is not to be suicide. Rather, it is God who kills the Christian, in order to bring him to life again.

The life to which God restores us is a life of communion with the Father. This communion, created by Christ the mediator between God and man, gives the Christian the freedom to be Christ's disciple. The life of discipleship then becomes easy, for as Christ says, "My yoke is easy, and my burden is light." (Matt. 11:30) Prayer is an essential part of this communion with God. Bonhoeffer says of this:

> If we are in communion with the Father, nought can harm us. We shall always be assured that he can feed his children and will not suffer them to hunger. God will help us in our hour of need, and he knows our needs.[44]

Bonhoeffer's Understanding of Prayer

God is the source of prayer, just as God is the source of faith and obedience. Just as true faith and true obedience are impossible without God's grace in Christ, so too is prayer impossible. Bonhoeffer writes that the order in the Christian life is "First, faith, then obedience." But faith is tied inextricably to obedience. One cannot claim to have faith and yet disobey God's commands. "The man who disobeys cannot believe, for only he who obeys can believe."[45] So the man who believes has faith, and because he has faith he obeys God's commands, one of which is also the command to pray. That prayer is one of the works to be done by the Christian is clear.

The disciples are given a share in this work, in the proclamation, in the defeat of Satan, and in intercessory prayer. If men cannot see this, they have as yet failed to discern the true nature of the service of the messengers of Jesus.[46]

Yet it is not the obedience of faith that gives prayer its power. "True prayer does not depend either on the individual or the whole body of the faithful, but solely upon the knowledge that our heavenly Father knows our needs."[47] If it were not for the great promises God has attached to prayer, it would be impossible for the Christian to come to God in prayer. So while it is the command to pray that drives the Christian to desire to pray, it is the promises of God that give the Christian the confidence to actually speak to God.

Prayer is the means of communion with each other. Only through Christ can we truly be connected to our neighbor. The life of the Christian is lived through the filter of Jesus Christ, the only mediator between God and man, and therefore Christ is the mediator between man and his neighbor as well. In intercessory prayer we go through Christ to reach our neighbor, just as we pray through Christ to God the Father. "The disciples are taught to pray, and so they learn that the only way to reach others is by praying to God."[48] Not only do we go through Christ to reach our neighbor, but in prayer we also become Christ to our neighbor. "One can become a Christ for one's neighbor through... intercession."[49] Bonhoeffer values intercession so much that he believes it to be more important even than praise and thanksgiving in prayer. "Thus the essence of Christian prayer is not general adoration, but definite, concrete petition."[50]

For Bonhoeffer, intercession lies at the heart of the prayer life of the Christian. But how should the Christian intercede? Indeed, what should she pray? Bonhoeffer is not a proponent of *ex corde* prayer, or prayer done whenever "the Spirit moves." Prayer, instead, should be shaped by the Scriptures - the Word of God - and should be a disciplined activity. We must learn to pray, using not "the false and confused speech of our hearts but the clear and pure speech, which God has spoken to us in Jesus Christ."[51] Reading and learning the Scriptures is a key part of learning to pray. In fact, Scripture reading should always immediately precede prayer, as it does in worship. Only when we have heard God's word to us can we adequately speak to God. "Scripture meditation leads into personal prayer."[52] Praying Scripture, especially the prayers given by God, is the surest way for the Christian to know she is praying rightly, as God would have her pray. For example, Bonhoeffer values highly the Lord's Prayer. He writes, "The Lord's Prayer is not merely the pattern of prayer, it is the way Christians must pray. If they pray this prayer, God will certainly hear them."[53]

Prayer as Response to Christ's Call to Service

Bonhoeffer sees God chiefly as revealed in Jesus Christ, who in turn calls all people to obey him. God is not a transcendent, sovereign being who is waiting for a response - in prayer or otherwise - from the Christian before acting. Rather, God has acted and continues to act decisively in Christ. The Christian must, by faith, respond to the call of Christ to follow him. Chief among the acts of obedience that God calls from the Christian is prayer. He prays because God has commanded him to pray, and because God has promised to act on his prayers. The content of his requests should flow out of Scripture. Only the Word of God can properly shape the content of the Christian's prayers, and especially his intercessions. These intercessions should not be centered on himself, but on his neighbor. In fact, it is only through prayer that anyone can truly interact with his neighbor, because Christ is now the mediator not only between God and humanity but between all peoples as well.

Francis Pieper

Not long after Martin Luther's death, the task of systematizing Luther's doctrine was undertaken. By the 18th century, several Lutheran theologians has produced *Theological Commonplaces* describing in detail the doctrine taught by the Lutheran Church. In the late 19 century, one of the last of the theologians standing in this tradition produced his *Christliche Dogmatik*, or *Christian Dogmatics*. His name was Franz, or Francis Pieper. He served as a professor of the Lutheran Church - Missouri Synod, as well as serving as its president from 1899-1911. Pieper represents the dogmatic tradition of the Lutheran Church and its view of Christian prayer.

Who is Pieper's God?

Most of Pieper's Dogmatics is occupied with explaining the nature of God and his work in the world. As would be expected, Pieper's views reflect the prevailing orthodox Lutheran position of his day. This includes a belief in God's triune nature as explained in the first four ecumenical councils of the Church, as well as a belief in the two natures of Christ as defined at Chalcedon and further defined in the Lutheran Confessions, especially the *Formula of Concord* Article VIII. Pieper emphasizes God's attributes as well, including his omnipresence, omnipotence, and omniscience. As a divine monergist, Piper attributes the Christian's salvation to the work of God alone, but the damnation of the lost solely to his own works and decisions. In short, Pieper holds to an orthodox and traditionally Lutheran understanding of the nature and persons of God and of Christ.

Pieper's Understanding of Prayer

Pieper places discussions on prayer throughout his dogmatics. Pieper seems to recognize that prayer is a difficult topic to place, placing one discussion toward the end of his discussion of the Christian life, just before his section of the Christian hope of eternal life, and another at the end of his discussion on the means of grace. The first section deals with the aspect of prayer as the response of faith. The second section, under the means of grace, deals with the numerous theologians who have placed prayer alongside the Word and the Sacraments as a means of receiving the forgiveness of sins. The first and major section, dealing with prayer as an aspect of the sanctified life, will be discussed first, with Pieper's second section discussed subsequently.

The Christian is always in prayer. Pieper writes, "As soon as a Christian has been justified by faith... he begins to commune with God. This personal conversing of the Christian with God is called prayer."[54] Through the saving Gospel of Christ present in preaching, in Scripture, and in the Sacraments, the Holy Spirit creates faith and makes believers. The faith of the believer - her trust in God's gracious promises - is expressed to God through prayer. Since prayer is an expression of faith, and the Christian can at no time be lacking faith, or else cease to be a Christian, it follows that the Christian is always in prayer.

The content of prayer must be shaped by the will of God as revealed in Scripture, since this is the means by which God conforms the Christian's will to his. Since the Christian's will is so shaped, the Christian's prayer is necessarily an expression of God's own will for the world. Since God desires all men to be saved, the Christian prays that this may be so, and God's answer is his continued oversight and expansion of the Kingdom of God. Since God wishes justice among the nations, the Christian prays for justice, and God works through governments and their agents to bring justice to all people. Because of this, Pieper can say that God works through the prayers of Christians to do his work in the world:

Since the will of Christians as expressed in their prayers coincides with the all-sustaining and governing will of God, it follows that the Christians' prayer sustains and governs instrumentaliter the whole world. The prayer of Christians has its effect on all occurrences in the Church and the world.[55]

Nonetheless, Christians remain sinners in this world, despite being saints through the righteousness of Christ. The Christian does not know God's will as it pertains to the matters of this world and its temporal governance; that remains the hidden will of God. Therefore we are to pray conditionally for temporal matters. Yet the Christian knows the good and perfect will of God as it pertains to the spiritual and to salvific matters. The Christian can then pray unconditionallyfor spiritual matters.[56]

This leaves the matter of whether prayer, besides being obedient trust in God, is also a means through which the Christian receives God's grace. In Pieper's time, as in ours, this was a commonly held view by Reformed theologians and even some Lutherans. Methodists, Pieper notes, list "prayer, searching the Scriptures, the Lord's Supper, fasting, and Christian conference" as means of grace.[57] Pieper opposes this understanding of prayer as a means of grace on the grounds that it confuses the human's actions with God's actions:

Word and Sacrament are the means through which God deals with us men, that is, imparts to men the remission of sins earned by Christ and through this bestowal creates and strengthens faith in them... By prayer, on the other hand, the believers are doing something toward God. Prayer is an exercise of the faith of Christians. If now we coordinate prayer with Word and Sacrament as a means of grace, it can easily be regarded as a complement of the grace of God, as if

God became fully reconciled and ready to forgive men their sins by their work of prayer.[58]

Those who believe in a limited atonement want to include prayer as a means of grace to provide personal assurance to the believer of her salvation, since an objective assurance is not possible:

> They must rather refer sinners who are terrified of God's Law and are seeking grace to prayer and other human endeavors and by these activities induce in them such moods and feelings as can perchance be regarded as marks of sonship with God.[59]

Likewise, those holding to the free will of people in spiritual matters already teach that the gift of divine grace depends on what man does, and so including prayer alongside other good works as a means of grace makes perfect sense.

Pieper does understand the objections of those who would believe that prayer is a means of grace. Christ calls on us to ask, and it will be given to us (Matthew 7:7), and to seek forgiveness for our sins in prayer (Luke 11:4[a]). But it is not, in Pieper's view, the prayer that earns forgiveness but the faith from which the prayer arises that receives forgiveness in the Gospel. "Because Christians still sin," Pieper writes, "and this sin registers in their conscience as guilt, the faith still present in their hearts reacts... by fleeing to the gracious promise of the Gospel."[60]

Prayer as Conversation of the Heart with God

Pieper holds to a classic Lutheran view of God, his persons and his work, and so also holds to a classic Lutheran view of prayer. The

---

[a] ...and forgive us our sins, for we ourselves forgive everyone who is indebted to us. And lead us not into temptation." (Lk 11:4)

Christian prays continually because prayer is the expression of a true faith and trust in God and his Gospel. The Christian prays for those things which God desires; for peace and justice in the world, and for all people to hear and believe the Gospel. The former the Christian prays for conditionally, since God's will for the world is hidden from view. But the latter the ChristianAprays for unconditionally, for the Gospel is God's revealed and complete will for all people.

Pieper runs squarely into the difficulty presented by Luther's own writings and interpretation of the Scriptures: is prayer a sacrament or a work of the Christian? Pieper chooses to remain with a classic Lutheran understanding, that prayer is only work and not to be understood in any sense as a means of grace. Since Pieper sees prayer primarily as a "the conversation of the heart with God,"[61] he does not deal with the presence of the Word of God itself in prayer and how that may or may not change the relationship of prayer to the traditional means of grace, chiefly the Gospel as present in the Scriptures. By making prayer "wordless," he avoids having to deal with the Scriptures being a means of grace when heard, but not necessarily when heard out of one's own mouth. Pieper limits prayer to the actual communication of the believer with God.

Conclusion

The five authors examined here represent well the breadth and depth of the Lutheran tradition. All of them, when speaking of God, focus much of their attention on Christ rather than on an abstract and transcendent deity for which Christ is merely the doorkeeper. Wangerin is the weakest in this regard, with Bonhoeffer and Hallesby being the most Christ-centered in their God language. This seems in keeping with Wangerin's liberal tradition, and Bonhoeffer and Hallesby's pietistic Lutheran roots. All the authors focus on God's love in Christ, and the promises he has made in association with prayer, as being foundational for the possibility of prayer.

Without God's having reconciled us to himself in Christ, true prayer could not occur.

As for the content of prayer, all the authors agree that intercessory prayer is not only possible, but commanded. This opinion is not arrived at from theological deduction, but from the Biblical witness. If God has promised to answer our prayer, and commanded us to pray, then our intercessions must be of value. No author sees this as infringing on God's sovereignty, but as God working through the Body of Christ in the world, of which all Christians are a part. The content of intercession is also derived from Scripture, and focuses both inward and outward. In terms of focusing inward, prayer is seen chiefly as request for a strengthening of faith and conformity with God's will. Each of the individual authors' inclinations appear in the matter of the outward focus of prayer. Fryar, who in her book tends to sound the most like a member of the Evangelical sub-culture, emphasizes mission and expansion of the Kingdom of God. Wangerin emphasizes care and consideration for others, and the strengthening of family and community, and our relationship with God. Bonhoeffer is more intent on praying for justice and peace. Hallesby sees prayer as the means whereby we open our heart to God. Pieper, lastly, sees prayer chiefly as the commune of the called and redeemed soul with God.

In conclusion, it seems that the central idea of prayer as an expression of trust in God in all things, especially for salvation, is not entirely lost in contemporary Lutheran writings. However, the idea of prayer as spiritual experience (Hallesby, Wangerin), as a Christian obligation (Bonhoeffer) and as a means of expanding the Kingdom of God on earth and experiencing a richer spiritual life (Fryar) are also present. And so other ideas of prayer have also found their way into Lutheran thought. The connection between faith and prayer, unfortunately, tends to be lost as the other meanings are introduced.

Prayer remains an expression of faith, certainly. But it also becomes merely another good work, or a means to an end, or a means of grace. Pieper alone stresses prayer as a response of faith to the God who has saved the sinner.

---

[1] *Lutheran Cyclopedia.* Eriwn Lueker, ed. (Saint Louis: Concordia Publishing House, 1975, c1954).
[2] O. Hallesby. *Prayer.* Clarence J. Carlsen, trans. (Minneapolis: Augsburg, 1931), 39.
[3] Hallesby, 62.
[4] Hallesby, 165.
[5] Hallesby, 12.
[6] Hallesby, 171.
[7] Hallesby, 167.
[8] Hallesby, 167.
[9] Hallesby, 12.
[10] Hallesby, 166.
[11] Hallesby, 38.
[12] Hallesby, 155.
[13] Hallesby, 155.
[14] Hallesby, 103.
[15] Hallesby, 103.
[16] Hallesby, 63.
[17] Hallesby, 35.
[18] Hallesby, 45.
[19] Hallesby, 106.
[20] Walter Wangerin. *Whole Prayer.* (Grand Rapids, MI: Zondervan, 1998), 171.
[21] Wangerin, 26.
[22] Wangerin, 31.
[23] Wangerin, 32.
[24] Wangerin, 64.
[25] Wangerin, 105.
[26] Wangerin, 103.
[27] Wangerin, 206.
[28] Wangerin, 41.
[29] Wangerin, 143.
[30] Wangerin, 37.
[31] Wangerin, 145.
[32] Wangerin, 164.
[33] Jane Fryar. *Armed and Dangerous.* (Saint Louis: Concordia Publishing House, 1997), 13.
[34] Fryar, 14.
[35] Fryar, 69.
[36] Fryar, 163.
[37] Fryar, 14.
[38] Fryar, 84.
[39] Fryar, 87.
[40] Fryar, 114.
[41] Fryar, 125.
[42] Fryar, 125.

[43] Dietrich Bonhoeffer. *The Cost of Discipleship.* (New York: MacMillan Company, 1963, c1937), 99.

[44] LeFevre, 201.

[45] Bonhoeffer, 73.

[46] Bonhoeffer, 232.

[47] Bonhoeffer, 183.

[48] Bonhoeffer, 208.

[49] LeFevre, 78.

[50] Bonhoeffer, 183.

[51] LeFevre, 83.

[52] LeFevre, 87.

[53] LeFevre, 184.

[54] Francis Pieper. *Christian Dogmatics, Vol. III.* (Saint Louis: Concordia Publishing House, 1953), 77.

[55] Pieper, 80.

[56] Pieper, 82.

[57] Pieper, 215.

[58] Pieper, 216.

[59] Pieper, 218.

[60] Pieper, 217.

[61] Pieper, 77.

Chapter 6: How Lutherans Pray

No two personages were as important to Reformation doctrine as were Martin Luther and John Calvin. In one way or another, all Protestant Christians are heirs of one theologian or the other, and are usually mixed descendents of both. Since this is the case, the different approaches of Luther and Calvin to the Christian life and the Christian's relationship to God will be determinative, in some sense, for how many Christians now understand prayer. Calvin and Luther's approaches to Christianity will, in turn, help shape a discussion of the theologies of prayer discussed in the preceding chapters.

Luther viewed the Christian life as one of constant battle against sin, death, and the devil. Luther explains that Baptism indicates "that the Old Adam in us should by daily contrition and repentance be drowned and die with all sins and evil desires."[1] Only then can the new man arise to live before God in holiness and righteousness: a holiness and righteousness already possessed through Christ, but which is also hidden with him (Colossians 3:3[a]). Calvin, in contrast, was more interested in the new man living the righteous life here and now. For Luther, the old nature was a constant foe to be battled; for Calvin, the old nature seems to be far less of a threat. For Calvin, "The emphasis is on the help we need to be good Christians in our behavior, vs. Luther, where the emphasis is on the need for help in saving us from 'false belief, despair, and other great shame and vice.'"[2] Luther possessed a negative view of Christian ethics, over against nascent Calvinism and its slightly more positive attitude. One might summarize these positions by saying that the Lutheran is

---

[a] For you have died, and your life is hidden with Christ in God. (Col 3:3)

constantly putting his old flesh to death; the Calvinist constantly urging his new creation to better life.

These two differing approaches to the sanctified life also impacted their approach to prayer. For Luther, the stress was on prayer as confession of sin and petition to do better. For Calvin, confession is minimized and prayer becomes more centered on the request for the power to live a decent Christian life. For both Luther and Calvin, prayer flowed out of the Scriptures, since it was there that one found the revelation of God's will. However, Luther's understanding of the Scripture was as a revelation of God's salvation, while for Calvin it was a guide for the living of a righteous life. What this means is that the true heirs of Luther focus on the salvific relationship with God in prayer; the heirs of Calvin focus on the life they are living and its constant improvement. Since this is the case, prayer literature consistent with Calvin's position is more focused on the living of life on earth as God would desire it. In contrast, Lutheran literature focuses more on what God has done and is continuing to do in us and for us through Christ, the Savior.

It has been argued that the quest for an improved sanctified life can be sought in three areas. The first is moral, as taken up by Kant and his quest for a religion of pure morality. In this case, prayer becomes part and parcel of the need for a Christian to behave ethically in the world. The second is spiritual, as represented by Schleiermacher and his quest for a "spiritual" religion. For Schleiermacher, prayer is a means of coming into contact with the All, and nurturing the spirit within. The last is communal, or covenant, as represented by Barth and his return to a more traditional form of Christianity. Barth represents those Christians who would retain a more traditional view of prayer, but especially emphasize the need for the Christian to live a life of justice in the world.

Of the views on prayer have examined here, Fox's falls most clearly into the tradition of religion as morality. Certainly there are a great number of authors, as mentioned in Chapter 4, who propound a religion of pure morality. For all these writers, prayer is nothing but the Christian (or religious person's) action in the world. Prayer to a sovereign God has no value. Like Rousseau in *Émile*, this group of theologians sees prayer as asking God for what he has already given us: free will to promote justice and mercy throughout the world. This theme is taken up in Bonhoeffer's writings as well, although he falls more clearly into Barth's orthodox, covenantal approach to prayer. Bondi also emphasizes prayer as action, not simply a "talking to God" about subjects of which he is already aware.

The Pop Evangelicals fall most clearly into the Schleiermachian tradition of spiritualizing the sanctified life. There is little in their writing about intercession for others, beyond immediate family and friends, and of course intercession for the mission of the church. The chief concern for the Pop Evangelicals is acquiring God's spiritual blessings, especially a "feeling" of connectedness with God. This is not to say that these Evangelicals have abandoned the notion of a personal God, as Schleiermacher did. They certainly refer to the Scriptures when discussing God's nature and being. But like Schleiermacher, they defined God without really relating that God to Christ. They also tend to see prayer as a means of grace, at least a means of establishing a relationship with Christ and maintaining that relationship. Pieper comments on this trend, quoting another author as stating, "It is confusing and to be rejected when recent theologians, following Schleiermacher... classify also prayer in the name of Jesus with the means of grace."[3] Wangerin, being of a more liberal Lutheran bent, also tends in this direction, as does Hallesby. Wangerin sees prayer as including communication from God, and Hallesby speaks of prayer as the means of allowing the Spirit's entry into the doorway of the heart. In the end, these views are not all that different from the "spiritual exercises" of the Jesuits. "For the Catholic, meditation and spiritual exercises are self-preparation for the reception of spiritual graces. According to Ignatius Loyola, the worshiper thus co-operates with God, serves God, and saves his soul."[4]

Last, we find those who, like Barth, wish to retain some traditional Christian dogma, and stress Christ, but also focus more on the spiritual life towards one's neighbor than on the battle against sin. Into this group fall Lewis and Ellul, both of whom could be classified as classical Reformed theologians, although Lewis perhaps less so. Both Ellul and Lewis are intent on preserving the traditional understandings of God and the Christian faith. Both are not shy of speaking about sin. But the emphasis in their theologies of prayer is on asking God for help in living a renewed life. The emphasis is slight, but there nonetheless. Fryar also tends to emphasize prayer as a leading toward a better life, rather than as a means of fighting devil, world, and flesh.

What is lacking in most of these books, with but a few exceptions, is Luther's understanding of prayer as a radical trust in the God who most desires to save, not improve, life. Many of the authors lack a deep appreciation for the sinful condition, and what mortal danger Christians are in every day. Those who do have an appreciation for this condition, for example Hallesby and Bonhoeffer, turn prayer into part of a program to redouble our efforts, rather than emphasizing prayer as a falling on our knees before the only one who can rescue us from the bondage (Romans 7:25[b]). Fryar and Ellul both come close to this understanding, while never explicating it head on. At stake is the danger of turning Christ into a helper, rather than a

---

[b] Thanks be to God through Jesus Christ our Lord! So then, I myself serve the law of God with my mind, but with my flesh I serve the law of sin. (Ro 7:25)

redeemer. Worse yet, Christ may be lost altogether in the quest for a meaningful relationship with "God."

As is always the case in Lutheran thinking, Christ is and must always remain the center of all doctrine and practice. This is certainly no less true for prayer. We pray because we are commanded to, just as we are commanded to partake of the Lord's Supper, to partake of Baptism, and to listen to God's Word. By the actions themselves - eating, washing, listening - we do not earn what God delivers in them. But by faith we receive what God has promised to give us in each case. As for prayer, God has promised to hear our every request, and so we pray at all times.

When prayer becomes a self-centered enterprise, an intellectual exercise, or a work deserving of God's favor, Christ is diminished. The gift becomes a merit. At the center of a Lutheran prayer life must remain the need for Christ to forgive us and cleanse us, save us from the time of trial, and defend us from the Evil One. We ask for these things because they are those things for which Christ has told us to ask. To conclude in the words of Luther,

> Our petitions— peace in the world, wisdom for magistrates—are far inferior to a prayer for eternal life and remission of sins. Let everyone then expand his heart and pray not to a simple little God but to the God of the heaven and earth He created. So He will give great things to those who ask for great things. Christians who understand that these are the gifts of God pray. Let this be the first fruit of love: that you pray.[5]

---

[1] Martin Luther. *The Small Catechism*. (Saint Louis: Concordia Publishing House, 1986), 22.

[2] *A New Handbook of Christian Theology.* Donald W. Musser and Joseph L. Price, eds. (Nashville: Abingdon Press, 1992), 161.

[3] Francis Pieper. *Christian Dogmatics.* (Saint Louis: Concordia Publishing House, 1953), 215.

[4] John Doberstein. *Minister's Prayer Book.* (Minneapolis: Fortress, 1986), XII.

[5] Martin Luther. *Luther's Works: Vol. 28: 1 Corinthians 7, 1 Corinthians 15, Lectures on 1 Timothy.* Edited by Pelikan, Jaroslav Jan, Hilton C. Oswald, and Helmut T. Lehmann. Luther's Works (Saint Louis: Concordia Publishing House, 1999, c1973), 1 Timothy 2:1.

Selected Bibliography

The Writings of Martin Luther

Luther, M. "A Simple Way to Pray" in Vol. 43: Luther's works: Devotional Writings II. J. J. Pelikan, et al, eds. Luther's Works. Philadelphia: Fortress Press, 1999, c.1968

Luther, M. "Appeal for Prayer Against the Turks" in Vol. 43: Luther's works: Devotional Writings II. J. J. Pelikan, et al, eds. Luther's Works. Philadelphia: Fortress Press, 1999, c.1968

Luther, M. "Comfort for Women Who Have Had a Miscarriage" in Vol. 43: Luther's works: Devotional Writings II. J. J. Pelikan et. al, eds. Luther's Works. Philadelphia: Fortress Press, 1999, c.1968

Luther, M. "Confession Concerning Christ's Supper", in Luther's Works, Vol. 37: Word and Sacrament III. J. J. Pelikan, et. al, eds. Luther's Works. Philadelphia: Fortress Press, 1999, c1961.

Luther, M. "On the Bondage of the Will" in Vol. 33: Luther's works: Career of the Reformer III. Philip Watson et. al., eds. Luther's Works. Philadelphia: Fortress Press, 1999, c.1972

Luther, M. "Personal Prayer Books" in Vol. 43: Luther's works: Devotional Writings II. J. J. Pelikan et. al, eds. Luther's Works. Philadelphia: Fortress Press, 1999, c.1968

Luther, Martin. "Treatise on Good Works" in Vol. 44: Luther's Works: The Christian in Society I. J.J. Pelikan, et. al., eds. Luther's Works. Philadelphia: Fortress Press, 1999, c1966.

Luther, Martin. "The Small Catechism" in The Book of Concord : The Confessions of the Evangelical Lutheran Church. Theodore Tappert, ed. Philadelphia: Fortress Press, 2000, c1959.

Luther, Martin. "The Large Catechism" in The Book of Concord : The Confessions of the Evangelical Lutheran Church. Theodore Tappert, ed. Philadelphia: Fortress Press, 2000, c1959.

Luther, Martin. What Luther Says: A Practical In-Home Anthology for the Active Christian. Edwald Plass, ed. St. Louis: CPH, 1959

Background Works

Barth, Karl. Prayer: According to the Catechisms of the Reformation. Philadelphia: Westminster Press, 1952

Bondi, Roberta. Memories of God. New York: Abingdon Press, 1995

Calvin, John. Writings on Pastoral Piety. Elsie Ann McKee, ed. New York: Paulist Press, 2001

Carson, D.A, ed. Teach Us To Pray: Prayer in the Bible and the World. London: World Evangelical Fellowship, 1990

Doberstein, John. Minister's Prayer Book. Philadelphia: Fortress Press, 1986

Gonzalez, Justo. The Story of Christianity. Peabody, MA: Prince Press, 2001, c.1984

LeFevre, Perry. Understandings of Prayer. Philadelphia: Westminster Press, 1981

Lutheran Cyclopedia. Lueker, Erwin. L. ed. St. Louis: Concordia Publishing House, 1954

New Handbook of Christian Theology, A. Musser, Donald W. and Joseph L. Price, eds. Nashville: Abingdon Press, 1992

Osborne, Richard. Philosophy for Beginners. New York: Writers and Readers Publishing, 1992.

Scaer, David P. "Luther on Prayer" in Concordia Theological Quarterly Vol. 47 No. 4. (October 1983)

Schleiermacher, Friedrich. On Religion: Speeches to Its Cultured Despisers. John Oman, trans. New York: Harper and Brothers, 1958 c.1799

Simpson, Robert L. The Interpretation of Prayer in the Early Church. Philadelphia: Westminster Press, 1965

Tappert, Theodore G. The Book of Concord : The Confessions of the Evangelical Lutheran Church. Philadelphia: Fortress Press, 2000, c1959.

Contemporary Theological Works

Roberta Bondi, Memories of God. New York: Abingdon Press, 1995

Bondi, Roberta. To Pray and To Love: Conversations on Prayer with the Early Church. Minneapolis: Fortress Press, 1991

Ellul, Jacques. Prayer and Modern Man. C. Edward Hopkins, trans. New York: Seabury Press, 1970

Fox, Matthew. On Becoming a Musical, Mystical Bear: Spirituality American Style. New York: Paulist Press and Deus Press, 1976

LeFevre, Perry. Radical Prayer: Contemporary Interpretations. Chicago: Exploration Press, 1982

Lewis, C.S. Letters to Malcolm: Chiefly on Prayer. San Diego: Harvest Books, 1992, c.1964

Evangelical Works

Gothard, Bill. The Power of Crying Out. Sisters, OR: Multnomah, 2001

Hannegraf, Hank. The Prayer of Jesus. Nashville: Word, 2000

Hybels, Bill. To Busy Not To Pray. Downers Grove, IL: Intervarsity Press, 1988

Omartian, Stormie. Praying God's Will for Your Life. Nashville: Harvest, 2000

Wilkinson, Bruce. The Prayer of Jabez. Sisters, OR: Multnomah, 2000

Lutheran Works

Bonhoeffer, Dietrich. The Cost of Discipleship. New York: MacMillan
     Company, 1963, c.1937

Fryar, Jane. Armed and Dangerous: Praying with Boldness. St. Louis:
     Concordia Publishing House, 1997

Hallesby, Ole. Prayer. Clarence J. Carlsen, trans. Minneapolis:
     Augsburg, 1994, c.1931

Pieper, Francis. Christian Dogmatics. St. Louis: Concordia Publishing
     House, 1953.

Wangerin, Jr., Walter. Whole Prayer: Speaking and Listening to God.
     Grand Rapids, MI: Zondervan, 1998

Made in the USA
Middletown, DE
27 July 2022

70110261R00066